Ristorante Fellini

Ristorante Fellini

Italian Cooking at its Best

Tony Percuoco

NEW HOLLAND

First published in Australia in 2008 by
New Holland Publishers (Australia) Pty Ltd
Sydney • Auckland • London • Cape Town

1/66 Gibbes Street Chatswood NSW 2067 Australia
218 Lake Road Northcote Auckland New Zealand
86 Edgware Road London W2 2EA United Kingdom
80 McKenzie Street Cape Town 8001 South Africa

National Library of Australia Cataloguing-in-Publication entry

Percuoco, Tony.
Ristorante Fellini cookbook : Italian at its best / Tony Percuoco.

ISBN: 9781741106695 (hbk.)

Ristorante Fellini (Restaurant : Main Beach, Qld.) Cookery, Italian.

641.5945

Publisher: Fiona Schultz
Editor: Kay Proos
Publishing Manager: Lliane Clarke
Designer: Tania Gomes
Food Photography: Graeme Gillies
Back Cover and Incidental Photography: Tania Gomes
Cover Photograph: Getty Images
Production Manager: Linda Bottari
Printer: C&C Offset Printing Co (China)

10 9 8 7 6 5 4 3 2 1

Ristorante Fellini is at Marina Mirage, Main Beach, Queensland.

Dedication

I would like to dedicate this book to my late father, Mario Percuoco, who was my mentor and my inspiration for putting these recipes together. My siblings and I grew up watching him run the family restaurant; he was our teacher and a tower of strength. He loved food, but classical music and ballet, and live theatre and Italian literary works were also important factors in his life, and he was often writing verses and sketching. My father's love, zest for life and the way he used to philosophise, influenced my whole life and made me the man I am today.

Acknowledgements

I would like to thank my mother, Olimpia, who taught us cooking shortcuts and how to create wonderful dishes from simple ingredients.

Thanks also go to famiglia Percuoco: Armando, Anna, Carmela, Gianni, Carlo and all in the restaurant business, and to Gianni, who prints our menus. A final thanks to my other business partners Richard Burt and Raffaele Di Benedetto.

May God bless you, and *buon appetito*!

Contents

Italian Food: A Way of Life

Italian food is more than garlic, oil, pasta and pizza; it's a way of life. From morning until night, the day is filled with food and drink—preparing meals, eating with family, meeting in restaurants.

I have always been surrounded by food and cooking. My mother and father ran a restaurant in Naples and it seemed inevitable that I would end up working in the same business. It will never cease to amaze me that no written record of the dishes served in our parents' restaurant was ever kept, but both Mum and Dad were walking culinary dictionaries. Our Sunday lunches together were always spent talking and arguing about food and service. Finally, with this book, I can record my parents' recipes!

For Italians, the day always includes coffee; a very important part of the daily routine. We usually wake up to a large cup of caffé latte. (Or perhaps if we have had a night of strenuous lovemaking we may need some *zabaglione*, affectionately known as our eggnog, which is the best pick-me-up ever!) Mid-morning and throughout the day we enjoy an espresso or a ristretto (half a short black). We only have cappuccino or caffé latte for breakfast (never after dinner!).

Breakfast usually consists of breads, jam, butter, honey, pastries fresh juices and milk with coffee— with either freshly baked bread or *cornetti* (croissants) to dip into it.

Above: *My grandmother Raffaela Di Bitonto with my mother Olympia at a function.*

In Naples, where I grew up, we sat down for lunch at two o'clock. As you ate, different providores with pushcarts walked the streets selling all kinds of food: fresh ricotta cheese served in bamboo containers and freshly roasted hot peanuts. People lowered baskets from their balconies and the providore filled them with whatever he was selling. There are so many different food sellers you could almost shop from home.

But often lunch is spent in the local trattoria or *tavola calda* (fast food eateries), consuming either an antipasto, some bread or a plate of pasta, coupled with a couple of glasses of wine. Literally 'before the meal', antipasto consists of cold cuts, meat or seafood cold or hot, cheeses, marinated and pickled vegetables. I've included the recipes Peasant's curly endive (see page 27) and Melanzana scarpone (see page 32) in this book for antipasto.

The afternoon is reserved for visiting friends or family. It is traditional to drop into the local pastry shop on the way to buy a mixture of cakes or biscuits to take with you as a gift. The day is generally spent eating. It does not finish there.

Early evening, we meet at a bar to have a campari and soda and discuss politics, religion and relationships—the three things that we never should talk about.

During the week the day ends with dinner, the main meal. We dine late, at around eight or nine o'clock.

Pasta is never served as a main course but as an entrée. Entrées can also be dishes like soups, mussels and octopus. There are two soups in Italy: those based on a clear meat consommé, to which pasta, rice, small ravioli, dumplings or eggs are added just before eating, and heavier ones for winter, based on vegetables, both fresh and dried.

A main course is always meat, fish or poultry, and is always accompanied by salad or vegetables. The meal finishes with cheese and fresh fruit. Dessert is reserved for either weekends or special occasions.

During the day, we mostly drink mineral water and maybe a glass of wine. For dinner we always have an aperitif—campari,

Vittoria
ESPRESSO MACHINES

Above: *My father Mario (left) and his colleague.*
Below: *My grandparents, Armando and Carmela Percuoco at their fiftieth wedding anniversary.*

cinzano, aperol—drinks that are very low in alcohol, wine with the main meal, and to finish a digestive herbal drink or *grappa*. Liqueurs like *sambuca*, *limoncello* or *galliano* are often served for special occasions or Sundays. We generally consume beer in summer or when we eat either pizza or fried food.

On a Sunday evening you might take a walk along the *lungo mare*, the seashore of the Bay of Naples, and as night starts to fall, all the outdoor eateries are festooned with lights. You might stop at small food stores: one selling *aqua di mummarella*, a spring water that is kept in terracotta urns with an abundance of fresh cut juicy lemons; another selling fresh steamed mussels with a hot spicy sauce over baked bread; another serving oysters that are opened in front of you and eaten raw with lemon juice.

The day concludes with gelato in huge cones filled with your favourite flavour. What a day! In Naples they say: 'Live today and don't worry about tomorrow.'

At Fellini, we cook my mother and father's traditional Italian recipes with a modern Australian twist. Even though we can't get the same prosciutto from Parma, the fresh fish from the cold waters of the Mediterranean or the warm waters of the Adriatic, or the tomatoes from the volcanic soil of Mount Vesuvius, the Australian ingredients I use are fresh and of a high quality. What a wonderful place I now call home!

It gives me great pride to pass my family recipes over to you. I hope that they will give you and your family the happiness and fond memories that they have brought our family for generations.

Tony Percuoco

The Flavours of Italy

Italy is a land of many regions, and even areas that are relatively close can have very different food, customs, wine, and even dialects. From north to south the flavours vary depending on what is grown there or fished from the sea. Wherever you are in Italy though, one aspect of food that doesn't vary is the importance of using fresh ingredients. Ingredients in full season deliver the most incredible taste sensation and ensure a perfect dish every time.

Now let me take you through the essential ingredients of Italian cuisine.

Herbs and spices

The main herbs used in Italian cuisine are sage, bay leaves, basil, rosemary, oregano, thyme, mint, and parsley. These are generally grown in little pots placed either in courtyards or balconies. Herbs used in dishes vary according to what is in season.

With spices, the main ones that are generally kept in pantries are saffron, nutmeg, cloves, pepper and juniper berries. The amount of either herbs or especially spices is kept to a minimum, only added to accentuate flavours of ingredients.

Cheeses

Italians are not as renowned as the French when it comes to cheeses but we do have almost as many varieties, one of the most famous one is the parmesan cheese, *parmiggiano di grana*. It is usually aged between 12 to 16 months and this is one cheese that we use for cooking. *Parmiggiano reggiano* is aged for a minimum of two years and is eaten after dinner with fruit. When it comes to parmesan cheese, I would definitely use the Italian ones.

The true mozzarella cheese is made from buffalo milk, and is only produced in the Campania and Abruzzi region in Italy. This is a delicious cheese that can be eaten either raw or cooked. Mozzarella has been in existence since the 1400s. The cheese was originally called 'mozza'. It is possible that the cheese could have been produced even earlier than this, as the buffalos that were needed for its manufacture were imported into Italy by the 'Longobardi' in the sixth century.

In most parts of the world, fresh mozzarella is produced from cow's milk, making it slightly heavier in consistency and not as milky has the buffalo milk-based mozzarella. These versions are still of very high quality.

The northern parts of Italy are known for the soft cottage style of cheese like fontina, that can easily melt while cooking. Other cheeses include goats, sheep milk and cheddars and of course not forgetting gorgonzola, our beloved blue vein cheese. My favourite is provolone—this is a cheddar style of cheese that can not be reproduced anywhere else.

Rice

Rice in Italy is eaten mainly in the north, usually in the form of risotto. It is also made into pilafs, where unwashed rice and stock are cooked together. I have included Sartu di riso (see page 99) here as an example. Good quality arborio rice is now widely available. When cooked it develops a most pleasant creaminess while still keeping its *al dente* (firm) quality. Risotto in Italy is often served by itself as a first course or as an accompaniment to a main course.

Pasta

Good pasta must be made from durum wheat or it will stick and swell when cooked. Pasta comes in a hundred different shapes and sizes, and can be fresh or dried. When it comes to fresh pasta I would definitely recommend making your own, so I have included a recipe just for that. My preference is for dried pasta, because it will retain firmness during cooking, and will be easier to digest. After cooking your pasta in abundant salted water to *al dente* (firm), strain, and mix with your favourite sauces or condiments.

Vegetables

One of the most important things is to use fresh seasonal produce. These days a lot of vegetables are grown in controlled environments, glasshouses or hydroponically. While this often results in beautifully looking vegetable, it is pumped up with water and tasteless. Naturally or organically grown vegetables have a much higher concentration of flavour. The vegetables mainly used are eggplant, zucchini, capsicum, fennel, artichokes, lots of green leafy vegetables, tomatoes and root plants like beetroot, potatoand carrots are very important in casserole baked style dishes.

For most dishes the vegetable plays a secondary or, if you like, supporting role in all the ingredients or even the meals. It is always enhanced with dressing or herbs to extend the flavours.

We were always at the beach. Here I am between my sisters Carmela (left) and Anna.

Meat

A large variety of meats are used in Italian cooking. *Scaloppine* is generally a thin slice of veal that has been tenderised. *Scaloppine alla caprese* (veal with eggplant) is a classic. Heavier meat dishes are served for dinner and poultry for lunch, including light game and feathered friends. As well as chicken, pheasants and quails are enjoyed in different regions of Italy.

There are other specialised dishes that include venison, pork and lamb. *Abbacchio*, for example, is a typical Roman dish of a milk fed suckling lamb that has not yet tasted grass and is killed when 20 days old, weighing no more than 10kg (20lb).

Rabbit and hare are also on the menu in different regions. These are marinated for hours and slow-cooked until tender.

Fish and Seafood

Italy is a peninsula surrounded by three seas—the Mediterranean, the Adriatic and the Aegean. Of course fresh fish and seafood feature prominently in the cuisine. I try to cook my fish and seafood in the simplest manner possible so as not to bury the delicious sea flavour in sauces and lengthy preparations. Fish is mainly served with a fresh green salad, never with chips and rarely with cooked vegetables.

Fish is mainly served as a main course. Some shellfish is served as an entrée, for example mussels, oysters, or bay shrimp. Seafood can also be included in risottos and with pasta.

A few simple rules apply when buying seafood—the eye of the fish should not be cloudy, the skin not slimy and it should definitely be firm to the touch. Try to smell the fish close to the bone as this is the first part to start smelling or discolouring when it's going bad. When smelling fish think of a time when you have taken a walk along the beach and enjoyed the fresh scent of salty seaspray in your nostrils—it should smell that good!

What's on the Menu?

Antipasto

Antipasto

This dish is perfect as part of an antipasto platter but also makes a great filling for focaccia. It is mostly served cold. A riesling or unwooded chardonnay should be served with this.

Endivia cafone

Peasant's curly endive

Serves 4

- Extra virgin olive oil
- 2 garlic cloves
- 2 chillies, chopped
- 50g (2oz) pine nuts
- 50g (2oz) sultanas
- 50g (2oz) capers
- 50g (2oz) black olives
- 500g (1lb) curly endives, washed
- Salt and black pepper, to taste
- White wine, splash

In a frying pan, heat olive oil and add whole garlic cloves. Fry until golden brown, add chilli and pine nuts and cook until golden brown.

Add sultanas, capers and olives.

Add the endive, season with salt and splash a little wine into the pan, place a lid on and steam for 3 minutes.

Continue to cook endive over a moderate heat without the lid for about 5 minutes. After most of the liquid has evaporated place on a serving plate and season with black pepper.

Every time I have a dinner party I always make a frittata. At other times I use leftover pasta to make one for a picnic or for when I am trekking through the bush taking pictures. You can also use zucchini, or onion—just let your imagination run wild. A frittata is a good accompaniment to any meat or fish dish.

Frittata di cipolle

Onion tart

Serves 6

- Olive oil
- 500g (1lb) Spanish onions, peeled and cut into fine strips
- Salt and pepper, to taste
- 2 bay leaves
- 6 eggs
- ¼ bunch continental parsley
- 50g (2oz) grated parmesan cheese

Place a small amount of oil in a non stick frying pan, when hot add your onions and sauté, stirring frequently. Add salt, pepper and bay leaves. When onions are soft and a rich golden colour place them in a colander and discard the bay leaves.

In a bowl, mix together the onions, eggs, parsley and parmesan cheese.

In the same frying pan add approximately 10ml (1/3 fl oz) of oil and the mixed ingredients. Cook over a moderate heat, not stirring contents of pan for one or two minutes, so that the bottom will set. Finish cooking the frittata in a moderate oven, 180°C (350°F) Gas Mark 4 for approximately 15 minutes or until the top becomes a lovely, dark, rich golden colour. Allow to cool.

When cold, run a spatula along the bottom and tip contents onto a round plate. This dish is generally served cold.

Previous page left: *Peasant's curly endive and* Right: *Onion Tart*

Frittata di zucchine

Zucchini tart

Serves 6

- Olive oil
- 500g (1lb) medium sized zucchini (courgette), cut into thick rings
- salt and pepper, to taste
- 6 eggs
- ½ bunch continental parsley
- 50g (2oz) parmesan cheese, grated

Place a small amount of oil in the pan, when hot add your zucchini, sauté stirring frequently, add salt and pepper.

When zucchini are soft and a rich golden in colour place them in a colander.

When cold, put zucchini in a bowl, add eggs, parsley and cheese. Mix together.

Now in the same frying pan add approximately 10ml (1/3 fl oz) of oil and fry the mixed ingredients.

Cook over a moderate heat, not stirring contents of pan for one or two minutes, so that the bottom will set.

Finish cooking the frittata in a moderate oven, 180°C (350°F) Gas Mark 4 for approximately 15 minutes or until the top becomes a lovely, dark, rich golden colour. Allow to cool.

When cold, run a spatula along the bottom and tip contents onto a round plate. This dish is generally served cold.

Scarpone means old boot, don't ask me where these names come from, but when you finish the dish I suppose it resembles an old boot. This is a very old recipe; eggplants were introduced to Italy from China or India in the late 1400s to early 1500s by the Arabs. Like all vegetables it is very low in calories or fats, but is often prepared fried and full of other fatty ingredients, so it is not a diet food. When combined with other foods, it has a particularly tangy flavour that I adore. This can either be served as part of an antipasto platter or as an entree.

Melanzana scarpone

Baked eggplant

Serves 4

2 large eggplants (aubergines)
Vegetable oil for frying
2 whole cloves of garlic, peeled
40g (1½oz) capers
40g (1½oz) olives pitted
4 large plum tomatoes, crushed or salsa pomodoro (see page 85)
Salt and pepper, to taste
¼ bunch fresh basil
40g (1½oz) parmesan cheese
40g (1½oz) breadcrumbs

Leaving the skin on, cut eggplant in half lengthwise, scoop the inside out and reserve.

Fry the eggplant boat in abundant oil, then leave on a paper towel to drain off excess oil.

Cut the scooped out flesh into small squares, sauté with garlic and oil, add capers, olives, and tomato, season and cook for 5 minutes, add the basil, parmesan cheese and a little breadcrumbs.

Transfer the mixture into the eggplant shell.

Place into baking dish with a little water, sprinkle breadcrumbs over the top and bake in a pre-heated hot oven, 200°C (400°F) Gas Mark 5 for 20 minutes.

Serve with fresh parmesan cheese and salsa pomodoro.

Parmiggiana has a place in every Neapolitan home and restaurant but the origin of this dish seems to be from Capri. Sweet, layered eggplant; you could almost call it vegetarian lasagna. If you don't use the whole lot (and you should always make extra) refrigerate it and eat it the next day, straight out of the fridge between 2 slices of bread, believe me you won't taste anything quite like it.

Some recipes put egg on top before baking it, I much prefer it my way, but then again, if you don't try, you won't know. This dish can be served hot or cold, as part of an antipasto platter or as an entrée.

Parmiggiana di melanzana

Eggplant lasagna

Serves 6

- 5 large eggplants (aubergines)
- Vegetable oil
- Plain flour
- 300g (9½oz) peeled tomatoes, crushed or salsa pomodoro (see page 85)
- 50g (2oz) parmesan cheese
- 100g (3½oz) mozzarella cheese
- 1 bunch fresh basil
- Salt and pepper, to taste

Peel and cut eggplant into slices (lengthwise), ½cm (¼in) thick. Salt the slices and leave them in a colander so that the water can drain (also to take any bitter taste out of them).

Pour oil into a heavy frying pan and let it heat up. Dust eggplant lightly on both sides with the flour, then fry the eggplant, turning over to cook both sides, until they are golden brown.

Place fried eggplant on absorbent towel to drain. On a platter, spread a thin layer of salsa pomodoro, place an even layer of eggplant on top, then add second spread of sauce followed by sprinkled parmesan cheese. Randomly place thin slices of mozzarella and ripped fresh basil leaves over this.

Cover with another layer of eggplant and repeat process for 3 to 4 layers, to personal taste. Finish the dish with a spread of the sauce and parmesan cheese. Bake in a slow oven, 150°C (300°F) Gas Mark 2 for 20 minutes.

In Italy this is a treat for late summer and autumn when the capsicums have soaked up the sun. You can buy cheap capsicums for this since you are cutting them into pieces and frying them anyway (padella just means frying pan). This dish can be served hot or cold, as part of an antipasto platter or even to accompany meat.

Peperoni in padella

Pan-fried peppers

Served as antipasto or side dish

- 500g (1lb) large red and green capsicums (peppers)
- 100ml (3fl oz) extra virgin Olive oil
- 2 cloves garlic
- 50g (2oz) capers, washed
- 50g (2oz) black Ligurian olives, pitted
- Small bunch of continental parsley, roughly chopped
- Salt and pepper to taste

Cut capsicums in half and remove seeds and membrane. Wash and dry them with kitchen towel and slice into large squares.

Place a large frying pan over a high heat, heat oil and sauté the whole garlic and capsicum. Cook for 5 minutes, tossing the pan or stirring.

Now add the capers and olives, sauté lightly to amalgamate all the flavours. Cook, stirring frequently, for a further 5 to 6 minutes.

At the end, add your parsley to the pan and toss.

Peperoni al gratin

Gratin of peppers

Serves 4

4 capsicums (peppers)
80ml (2½fl oz) extra virgin olive oil
3 cloves garlic, chopped
¼ bunch parsley
60ml (2fl oz) water
50g (2oz) breadcrumbs

Roast the capsicum over a barbeque or open flame until the skin is blackened.

While still hot, peel the skin, cut out the membrane, remove seeds and cut into thick strips. You can also allow the capsicum to cool in a plastic bag where it will sweat and the skin will come off more easily. Under no circumstances should you put capsicums under running water—they will lose all their flavour.

In a bowl, combine capsicum with the oil, garlic, parsley and water.

Place in an oven dish in 1 layer and sprinkle the breadcrumbs evenly over the top. Cover with foil and place in a preheated slow oven, 150°C (300°F) Gas Mark 2 and cook for 20 minutes. Do not stir.

Left: *my taste for food started early.*

Lacto
Mellin

Olive Oil: The Lifeblood of Italy

Italy is one of the largest producers of olive oil in the world along with Spain, Greece, Morocco and Australia. In Italy, oil is produced in three states; Tuscany, Liguria, which produces the most refined and elegant olive oil and Puglia, at the tip of the boot of Italy close to Sicily, which is probably the largest producer. These regions all produce their extra virgin olive oil locally but when it comes to plain olive oil, olives grown in the south can be transported to the north then pressed and bottled under the Tuscan or Ligurian label.

Most olives are picked by hand. If the olives are too mature their acid levels are usually too high. Genuine extra virgin olive oil is made from the first pressing of olives which are ground in a couple of different ways, commonly with a stone wheel. Extra virgin oil must have an acidity level of below 1 per cent and no added preservatives. Very low acidity can also be achieved with the use of chemicals, so try and stay away from the large producers of olive oil; the smaller companies will usually place a lot more emphasis on the quality, rather than quantity.

Like wines that carry the DOC or DOCG labels (denomination of origin controlled and denomination of origin controlled and guaranteed), the words 'estate bottled' on an olive oil bottle usually means a higher quality of oil. My late father always said that the term virgin olive oil dated back to the time of the Roman

Empire, when only virgins were allowed to pick the fruit.

In the early 1950s and 1960s after World War II many Italians migrated to different parts of the world—to America, northern and southern Germany, England and Australia. Many were nostalgic for the tastes of the old country and planted olive trees wherever they could.

When the wine industry boomed, many olive trees were ripped up and replaced with vines. Now we are faced with a worldwide olive oil shortage and the price of this liquid gold will only rise. Many people are now putting their life savings into farms and trying to produce the best extra virgin olive oil. In the Mt. Avoca winery in the Pyrenees wine region of Victoria one family owns a few 25-year-old trees and, unfortunately for the rest of Australia, can only produce enough oil for their immediate use. When I sampled it it was served in a very simple glass decanter and was very cloudy. I poured a little on my side plate and began to dip some freshly sliced bread in it. The taste was a cocktail of bananas and macadamia and very low on acidity. Beautiful.

There are two ways of tasting olive oil—as above with a piece of bread and, for the brave ones, to drink it from a small teaspoon. If it tastes bitter or the back of your throat hurts, it is possible that the oil is off.

Yes, oil can go off. Oil should be stored in dark green bottles away from direct sunlight—many expensive oils come in a cardboard box as protection from harmful rays. Always check the expiry date on a bottle of oil and after it has been opened, keep it in your pantry with the lid on. Never refrigerate oil and don't refill an opened bottle with fresh olive oil—once opened it will slowly start to go slightly rancid or acidic.

My view is that extra virgin olive oil, unlike wine, cannot be kept for a long period of time, it should definitely be used very young. Use straight from the bottle on salads, in soups, over fish, pasta, veal, anything really—it is a great waste to cook with extra virgin olive oil.

Plain olive oil comes after a further pressing and refinement of the fruit used for the extra virgin. It can be used as a general purpose cooking oil and also for frying. I use a good vegetable or peanut oil to fry with and vegetable oil to make mayonnaise. I think olive oil can sometimes make food far too heavy—many chefs will disagree with me on this, but it's all a matter of personal taste.

Olive oil changes according to the pressing for a particular year—like wine there are good and bad years. When you buy a bottle of olive oil you should go to as much trouble as you would to find a good or exceptional bottle of wine—let's not forget, OILS AIN'T OILS!

Peperoni ripieni

Stuffed baked peppers

Serves 4

- 4 red capsicums (peppers)
- 60 ml (2fl oz) olive oil
- 2 cloves garlic, diced
- 1 eggplant (aubergine), diced
- 50g (2oz) black seedless olives, chopped
- 25g (1oz) capers, chopped
- 4 anchovy fillets, chopped
- 2 tomatoes, chopped
- ¼ bunch basil, chopped
- 50g (2oz) breadcrumbs
- Salt, to taste
- 50g (2oz) parmesan cheese
- 50g (2oz) mozzarella, diced
- Extra virgin olive oil, to serve

Cut the top off of the capsicums and take the seeds out. Sprinkle insides with salt and stand them upside down and let the water drain out.

In a frying pan, sauté the garlic in the oil, adding the eggplant, olives, capers, anchovies, tomatoes and basil.

Cook for 5 minutes, adding half of the breadcrumbs, season with salt. Transfer to a bowl, and add the mozzarella, parmesan and the rest of the breadcrumbs to thicken it up.

Fill the capsicums with the mixture to the top, then place upright in an oven dish, pour about 100ml (3fl oz) of water in the tray, cover tightly with foil or a lid. Bake in a pre-heated oven at 200°C (400°F) Gas Mark 5 for 20 minutes.

Place on a plate, drizzle with extra virgin olive oil and serve.

For this recipe you need 2 small octopus, if can't find them there is no problem in using 1 large one but larger ones take a little more time to cook. Your fish supplier will generally clean them for you and often they tumble them with salt to tenderise them. If you have a stone or marble top in your kitchen you can do it yourself, just bash the octopus against the stone. This works in two ways; you tenderise the meat and you take out your frustrations on the octopus instead of your partner! Enjoy.

Polpi all' insalata

Octopus salad

Serves 6

- 2 x 500g (1lb) octopus, cleaned
- 2 bay leaves
- ¼ bunch continental parsley, chopped
- 2 garlic cloves, finely sliced
- 100ml (3fl oz) white vinegar
- 2 lemons, juiced
- 100ml (3fl oz) extra virgin olive oil
- Salt and pepper, to taste

Wash the previously cleaned octopus under running water, leaving the skin on.

Bring 5 litres of water to the boil and add the bay leaves. Immerse the octopus and cook for 1½hours or until tender.

Drain, leave to cool in water, then cut into 3cm (1in) strips. Place in a bowl and add the parsley, garlic, vinegar and lemon juice, mixing well. Leave in the fridge for 30 minutes.

Prior to serving, taste then add salt (do not use salt while boiling the octopus) if needed and freshly ground pepper. Add the extra virgin olive oil.

For extra texture you can add fresh chopped celery to the salad.

Peperoni insalata

Salad of peppers

Serves 4

- 3 capsicums (peppers)
- Salt and pepper, to taste
- 3 cloves garlic, thinly sliced
- 2 lemons, juiced
- ¼ bunch parsley, chopped
- 80ml (2½fl oz) extra virgin olive oil

Roast the capsicum over a barbeque or open flame until the skin is blackened.

While still hot, peel the skin, cut out the membrane, remove seeds and cut into thin strips. You can also allow the capsicum to cool in a plastic bag where it will sweat and the skin will come off more easily. Under no circumstances should you put capsicums under running water—they will lose all their flavour.

Place in a mixing bowl, season then add the lemon juice, parsley, oil and garlic.

Transfer to a serving dish. Serve cold.

Pomodori inbottiti

Stuffed baked tomatoes

Serve as antipasto or side dish

- 16 vine-ripened tomatoes
- 100g breadcrumbs
- 10g (½oz) oregano (dried)
- Salt and pepper, to taste
- Extra virgin olive oil

Cut the tomatoes in half, take the pulp out and place it in a mixer with the breadcrumbs, oregano, salt, pepper. Blend, keeping the mix quite wet.

Spoon the mixture back into the tomatoes, sprinkle with breadcrumbs and oil.

Place in an oven tray with a little water in the bottom and bake in a pre-heated hot oven, 220°C (450°F) Gas Mark 6 for 15 minutes.

Zucchini alla scapece

Fried zucchini

Serve as antipasto or side dish

- 500g (1lb) medium-sized zucchini (courgette)
- Vegetable oil for frying
- 4 cloves garlic, thinly sliced
- Salt and pepper, to taste
- 1 bunch fresh mint
- 200ml (6½fl oz) white wine vinegar

Wash and slice the zucchini into thick rings. Half fill a pan with vegetable oil and fry them.

Place in colander to drain any excess oil and allow to cool.

In a bowl, add garlic, salt, mint and vinegar.

Toss in the zucchini, season and mix well so that they can absorb the flavours of the other ingredients.

Transfer on to a serving dish, leaving excess liquids behind. This dish is served cold.

Perfect Pasta

For many years now it has been said that Marco Polo brought pasta back from China in the 13th century. Well, I disagree with that because there are references to pasta that precede this, some of them from as far back as the Roman Empire. Also there is evidence that after the Arab invasion of the southern parts of Italy in the 8th century, dried pasta started to appear in the various regions. So the true origins of pasta are still somewhat of a mystery!

A lot of people today say that pasta is fattening—but it's not the pasta but the sauce that determines the fat content of the various dishes. Cooked pasta actually contains little fat and cholesterol. It is a good source of carbohydrates and provides our bodies with vitamins, minerals, energy and fibre. The nutritional value of pasta depends on which flour mix is used and its production.

Under Italian law, dry pasta can only be made from durum wheat which contains a higher level of protein (gluten) than bleached white flour and so makes the pasta much more elastic and able to hold its *al dente* (firm) characteristics. But you can make pasta at home from any type of flour, adding water and eggs and lots of different ingredients to it to make ravioli, fettuccine or any shape you desire.

Don't forget to 'laminate' the dough. The easiest way to do this is to buy a pasta machine that has two cylindrical stainless

saffron
lingu
ARTIGIANO
PASTAIO
fellini
pastificio fellini
AUSTRALIA
5-10min
or until “al dente” (firm)
25

steel rollers. When you pass the dough through these rollers, it makes it thinner. It is also important to allow the pasta time to rest before working with it.

The only similarity between locally produced and imported pasta is the fact that durum wheat is used. The differences are because of soil, water and climate, so you see it is not only the workmanship, which for obvious reasons is far more advanced in Italy than elsewhere, but also the actual raw product that might influence the flavour. The more arid and dry the soil, the better the end result, with less moisture and a more concentrated grain.

The planting and harvesting of durum wheat have similar characteristics to that of vine growing. Artisan pasta making, unlike the commercial type, is a process using less machines and more manual labour. The pasta is extruded through brass and not Teflon dies, making the surface rough, so that during cooking the sauce can coat the pasta more evenly. The drying of pasta is done at low temperature and over a long period of time compared to the commercial brands. A longer drying time means less time is needed to cook the pasta.

Ravioli di trota (see page 57) includes a recipe for homemade pasta. Remember when making your own pasta:

1. Use four times the amount of water to the amount of pasta.
2. As it comes up to a rapid boil, add the salt.
3. Always cook your pasta over a high heat.
4. Drain while it is still hard, don't overcook it.
5. Never refresh pasta under running water or place in a bowl with ice to stop it from over cooking, you will lose all the starch by doing so.
6. Try and always cook your pasta as you need it; pre-cooked pasta, even when stored in a refrigerator, can go rancid and tasteless.

Entrées

Entrées

Ravioli di trota

Trout ravioli

Serves 4

Pasta

500g (1lb) flour, sifted
3 eggs
Extra virgin olive oil
Pinch of salt
50ml of water

Make a well in the flour, place all the ingredients in the well and knead. Set aside to rest for a few hours. Roll out 2 sheets of pasta 1.5mm (.05in) thick. You can do this by hand or use a pasta machine with two cylindrical stainless steel rollers. Fold the dough about five or six times and pass through the rollers each time. Adjust the rollers to make it thinner each time. This is called laminating.

Filling

Extra virgin olive oil
2 bunches leeks , chopped
250g (8 oz) deep-sea ocean trout or fresh salmon, diced
Salt and pepper, to taste
100ml (3fl oz) sauvignon blanc
30 ml (1fl oz) fish stock
3 sprigs fresh thyme
2 egg whites
Pinch of saffron
1 egg, whisked

In a heavy-based frypan, heat the oil over a high heat and sauté the leeks. Add fish and seasoning then turn the heat to low and cook, stirring frequently.

Deglaze the pan with the wine and stock, and allow to reduce very slowly, adding the herbs at the end. Cool the ingredients, then blend in a food processor, ready to fill the pasta. Add the egg white

Place filling in even portions over 1 of the sheets, leaving gaps of approximately 4cm (1½in) between fillings. Repeat this process until you have filled up the sheet. Then place the other sheet over the top and cut out the ravioli, preferably with a serrated edge wheel. Brush the pasta on one side with the whisked egg.

This is good winter comfort food. The cheese gives you a different texture component when combined with the nuts. Preferably serve with a light red wine or even a blend, but if serving a white wine make it a rich chardonnay with some melolactic fermentation. One thing that you will notice about this dish is the absence of salt. I usually love to use a lot of salt to extract the natural flavours from ingredients, but here I would only add it to the egg wash because this should be a sweet, subtle dish.

Bocconcini al mascarpone

Mozzarella balls with mascarpone

Serves 4

- 12 bocconcini (mozzarella) balls
- Plain flour
- 3 eggs, beaten
- Breadcrumbs
- Vegetable oil for frying
- 80ml (2½fl oz) chicken or vegetable stock
- 250g (8 oz) mascarpone
- 125g (4oz) gorgonzola
- 80g (3oz) pistachio nuts, chopped
- Pepper, to taste

Drain the bocconcini and pat them dry with a tea towel. Dip in the flour, then the egg wash, then breadcrumbs.

In a frying pan, heat enough oil to come halfway up the balls. Fry the bocconcini, evenly coating them with the oil and turning to fry on all sides. Be careful not to overcook them or they will split. Then place on a tea towel to drain any excess oil and keep in a warm place.

In another pan, bring the stock to boil, adding first the mascarpone then the gorgonzola, reduce the sauce by half, stirring frequently.

Place the bocconcini on a serving plate or in individual dishes, pour the reduced sauce over them evenly and sprinkle over the nuts and pepper.

Capelli d'angelo é capesante

Angelhair pasta with fresh scallops

Serves 4

600g (1lb) 2 packets saffron angel hair pasta
30g (1oz) butter
1 leek, finely chopped
12 fresh scallops
Saffron, pinch
Salt and pepper, to taste
30ml (1fl oz) vodka
30ml (1fl oz) stock
30ml (1fl oz) cream
No cheese please

Cook the pasta in 6 litres of boiling salted water to *al dente* (firm) stage, stirring constantly.

Melt butter in a frying pan and add the leek. After few minutes add the scallops and saffron.

Cook over a medium heat, stirring frequently. Season with salt, add the vodka and fish stock. Reduce the sauce, add the cream and reduce again to a thick consistency.

Add to your drained cooked pasta, stir thoroughly, add some freshly ground pepper and serve.

For this dish you must use the freshest fish you can get, the fish is served raw it's the Italian version of sushi. A straight semillon would suit this dish.

Carpaccio di salmone é dentice

Marinated salmon and snapper

Serves 4

- 200g (6½oz) fillet of salmon
- 100g (3½oz) fillet of snapper
- 1 bunch onion chives
- 1 capsicum (pepper)
- Salt, to taste
- 2 lemons, juiced
- 40g (1½oz) capers, chopped
- ½ bunch basil, shredded (chiffonade)
- Extra virgin olive oil
- Freshly crushed pepper

Lightly season the inside of the salmon. Place the chives evenly over the salmon and lie the snapper on top. Wrap the salmon around the snapper to form a circular roll.

Wrap the roll tightly in cling film, freeze overnight.

Roast the capsicum over a barbeque or open flame until the skin is blackened. While still hot, peel the skin, cut out the membrane, remove seeds and cut into thin strips. You can also allow the capsicum to cool in a plastic bag where it will sweat and the skin will come off more easily. Under no circumstances should you put capsicums under running water—they will lose all their flavour. Place in a bowl.

Thinly slice the salmon and snapper roll with a slicer or sharp knife and arrange flat on a serving dish without overlapping the slices. Season with salt and lemon juice evenly to neutralise it then add the chopped capers, capsicum and basil, drizzle liberally with extra virgin olive oil and pepper.

Serve immediately.

Cozze al pomodoro

Rock mussels with fresh romato

Serves 4

- 100ml (3fl oz) extra virgin olive oil
- 3 cloves garlic
- 2 chillies
- 800g (1½lb) mussels (clams), cleaned
- 100ml (3fl oz) white wine
- 3 fresh tomatoes, chopped
- ½ bunch parsley, chopped

In a large pot, heat up the oil and add the whole cloves of garlic and the chillies.

Add the mussels, still in their shells, then cover with a lid to steam until they open—about 3 minutes.

Pour in the wine, making sure not to evaporate all the liquid and then add the chopped tomato. Cover pot with a lid.

Bring to the boil. Remove lid and cook for 10 minutes, add the chopped parsley, stir through and serve in a large bowl with crusty Italian bread to mop up the sauce.

Note

To clean mussels, place in a sink and scrape the shells of any foreign matter, then with a knife or tweezers pull out the beard at the flat part of the mussel.

Black rock mussels can often be found at the fish markets but are usually overlooked. When buying them, make sure that no bad odours are present and that they feel full in weight; when a mussel dies, it's not only light in weight, but the smell is unbearable. To clean mussels, place in a sink and scrape the shells of any foreign matter, then with a knife or tweezers pull out the beard at the flat part of the mussel.

Cozze ripiene

Stuffed mussels

Serves 4

1kg (2lb) mussels (clams)
100g (3½oz) breadcrumbs
50g (1½oz) parmesan cheese
¼ lemon, juiced
Extra virgin olive oil
3 cloves garlic, whole
100ml (3fl oz) dry white wine
3 vine ripened, plump tomatoes, chopped
½ bunch continental parsley, chopped

Place the mussels in a pot with lid to cover and steam for 2 minutes, until they open. Take them out of the pot and discard any closed ones. Reserve any water they might have thrown out.

In a bowl, mix the breadcrumbs, parmesan, lemon juice and a drizzle of oil. Half-fill the mussel shells.

In a frying pan, sauté the garlic with the oil then add the filled mussels. When partially cooked, pour in the wine along with any liquid that the mussels have thrown out.

Reduce for a few minutes, without letting the wine evaporate, then add the chopped tomato, chopped parsley, cover the pan and bring to the boil. (Do not at any stage add salt to this dish, if the mussels are fresh, they will contain a high level of natural sea salt.)

Transfer the cooked mussels to a serving platter leaving all the liquids in the pan, and over a high heat reduce the sauce and pour over the mussels.

Serve with grilled, crusty Italian bread.

Fettuccine di spinaci alle verdure

Spinach fettuccine with vegetables

Serves 4

- 2 packets (600g, 1¼lb) spinach fettuccine
- 50ml (2fl oz) olive oil
- 2 cloves of garlic, sliced
- 6 medium button mushrooms, sliced
- 1 small zucchini (courgette), sliced
- Salt and black pepper, to taste
- 1 punnet cherry tomatoes, halved
- 1 stem fresh basil leaves
- 50ml (2fl oz) extra virgin olive oil

Cook the fettuccine in 6 litres of boiling salted water to *al dente* stage (firm) stirring constantly.

While the pasta is cooking, heat the olive oil over high heat in a heavy pan large enough to fit the pasta. Add the garlic and sauté quickly. Add the mushrooms and zucchini and sauté for a couple of minutes. Season with salt and add the tomatoes. Cook until they just start to soften.

Add the basil leaves and the strained pasta with two tablespoons of water from the pasta. Pour over the extra virgin olive oil and stir through.

Serve finished with black pepper.

Fettuccine zafferano al salmone

Fettuccine with saffron and salmon

Serves 4

2 packets saffron fettuccine
2 tablespoons olive oil (for cooking)
2 cloves garlic
200g (6½oz) Atlantic salmon, chopped
80ml (2½fl oz) fish stock
1 punnet cherry tomatoes, halved
½ bunch basil, chopped
Black pepper, to taste
1 tablespoon extra virgin olive oil
No cheese please

Cook the fettuccine in 6 litres of boiling salted water to *al dente* stage (firm) stirring constantly.

In a heavy frying pan, heat up the oil over a moderate heat and fry the garlic, then add the salmon and tomatoes. Season and cook for 5 minutes.

Add the fish stock and reduce the sauce, then add it to the strained pasta.

Serve with the chopped fresh basil and pepper, finishing the dish with the extra virgin olive oil. You can grind some freshly milled black pepper over the dish.

Fettuccine al pollo

Fettuccine with chicken

Serves 4

- 50g (2oz) butter
- ½ bunch of shallots (spring onion, scallions), chopped
- 300g (9½oz) chicken breasts, chopped
- Salt and pepper, to taste
- 100ml (3fl oz) chicken stock
- 150ml (5fl oz) thickened cream
- 2 packets (600g, 1¼lb) fettuccine
- 1 avocado, diced
- parmesan cheese

In a heavy frying pan melt the butter and add the shallots. Cook for a few minutes then add the chicken and season.

Cook over a moderate heat, adding the first stock then the cream and reduce by half until it reaches a thick consistency.

Cook the fettuccine in 6 litres of boiling, salted water to *al dente* stage (firm), stirring constantly.

Combine the strained pasta, sauce and diced avocado. Sprinkle with parmesan and serve.

This is a dish which is readily available in Sicily and the southern parts of Italy where the whitebait are harvested in the warm waters of the Mediterranean. You can use New Zealand whitebait when it is in season, otherwise this is one of the only dishes that I would use frozen white bait in because it is consistent all year round. A semillon with a bit of age goes perfectly with this dish.

Frittelle de alici

Whitebait fritters

Serves 4

- 250g (8oz) whitebait
- 50g (2oz) plain flour
- 25g (1oz) parmesan cheese, grated
- 2 eggs
- ¼ bunch of continental parsley, chopped
- Salt and pepper, to taste
- Oil for frying
- 2 lemons, some juiced, some cut into wedges

In a bowl combine whitebait, flour, parmesan, eggs, half the parsley and the seasoning using a wooden spoon; the consistency should be quite runny.

In a frying pan, heat the oil over a high heat, only using enough oil to cover half of the frying pan.

Using a large spoon, add a heaped spoonful of battered whitebait into oil and fry to golden brown on both sides.

Place on a paper towel to drain any excess oil.

Transfer to a serving plate and top with salt, lemon juice, sprinkle with the remaining parsley, some black pepper and serve with a wedge of lemon.

MUSHROOMS:
Funghi trifolati

One of the particular dishes that I am very fond of to this day, and that almost got me grounded for life, is *funghi trifolati.*

I was all of ten years old and mum had just finished buying the food for Christmas. The kids were in the kitchen while she was putting it away and due to the rush of the day there wasn't much time to prepare lunch. So, we grabbed a rather large loaf of bread and she filled it with freshly sliced prosciutto, provolone and the most succulent artichokes.

These had been preserved the previous year in extra virgin olive oil with dried oregano and a hint of chilli, so you can just imagine the flavour of that *tramezzino.* Definitely not your average sandwich, a *tramezzino* needs Italian crusty bread (ciabatta) to soak up any juices or oils from the food. There was only one slight problem, it was a large loaf but I had to share it with my brothers and sisters.

Meanwhile, mum began to prepare for the Christmas Eve dinner— *funghi trifolati.* Mushrooms are generally very expensive in Italy at Christmas time and fresh herbs are almost nonexistent, so mum was very happy to find all these ingredients in the cool rooms at the restaurant.

I took up my usual place next to her, patiently waiting to attack the frying pan with a fresh piece of bread to mop up all the pan juices. My sisters were too busy being teenagers (I don't know what

The mushroom thief, aged 10

they were doing) and my brothers were too young to appreciate it. Sadly when she had finished cooking the mushrooms she put them away.

The aroma that those mushrooms left in that kitchen was almost killing me, so off I went on the hunt to try to find them. When I finally did, I honestly just meant to take a little bit off the top, but a little became more and more until I'd eaten half. By this stage the oil and natural juices were soaking the bread with the most incredible woody, yeasty flavours imaginable. On I went until there was nothing left.

Ah well, I thought, what can possibly happen to me over a plate of mushrooms? I'll tell you what happened—ouch—that hurt! My only regret is that I ran out of bread halfway through!

Funghi trifolati

Oil
Garlic clove, sliced
Button mushrooms, sliced
Salt
Continental parsley, chopped

Take a very large, heavy frying pan, coat it with a generous amount of olive oil and get it very hot. Add garlic and mushrooms, sauté and stir frequently, adding a generous amount of salt to bring out all the oil and water that is sucked in when mushrooms cooked.

As the mushrooms turn brown, add a generous amount of parsley. Remove from the pan with a perforated spoon leaving the remainder of the oil behind or maybe use a bit of bread to mop this up and eat instantly! Do not add any extra oil during cooking as this may turn your mushrooms slightly rancid. And make sure that Tony is not around if you hide them in your pantry.

This dish would best be served as an entrée, with perhaps a pinot noir. Some fresh rocket tossed in oil for garnish would give you a good peppery finish.

Funghi al forno

Baked portobella mushrooms

Serves 4

- 50g (2oz) pine nuts
- ½ bunch rosemary
- ½ bunch thyme
- ½ bunch sage
- 50g (2oz) oven roasted tomatoes
- 4 large portobella mushrooms (or large field)
- 25g (1oz) chopped onion
- 50g (2oz) breadcrumbs
- 600ml (20fl oz) extra virgin oilve oil
- Salt and pepper, to taste
- 100ml (3fl oz) chicken stock
- 100ml (3fl oz) cream
- 50g (2oz) gorgonzola

Separate the mushroom tops from the stalks. Chop up and combine the pine nuts, rosemary, thyme, sage, tomatoes, mushroom stalks and onion in a bowl. Add the breadcrumbs and drizzle some oil over to bind.

Oil a flat oven tray, place the mushrooms caps on it, sprinkle them with salt and oil, coat the mushrooms evenly with the mixture, and cook in a pre-heated oven 180°C (350°F) Gas Mark 4 for 15 minutes, do not burn the top.

In a frying pan over a high heat bring to the boil the stock, cream and gorgonzola, reducing to a thick consistency.

Place the hot mushrooms on serving or individual plates, pour the reduced sauce over them and serve with freshly milled black pepper.

This is an ideal dish for vegetarians. I simply love mushrooms—any variety, shape or size, they are so full of flavour.

Funghi alla griglia

Grilled field mushrooms

Serves 4

- 4 large field mushrooms or equivalent field mushrooms for 200g (6½oz) each
- 100ml (3½fl oz) garlic infused extra virgin olive oil
- ½ bunch parsley, chopped
- 2 lemons, juiced
- 100ml (3½fl oz) extra virgin olive oil
- Salt, to taste
- Black pepper, to taste

For garlic-infused olive oil: place whole cloves of garlic in a bottle with oil and leave for at least 2 days in a dark pantry to infuse the flavour of the oil.

Place mushrooms on an oiled oven-proof tray, season with salt, top with oil and place in a moderate oven, 180°C (350°F) Gas Mark 4 for approximately 10 minutes. The mushrooms are cooked when they start to sizzle.

Remove from the oven and place on either the char or flat grill. If using a char grill, turn the mushrooms to give cross markings.

Mix equal parts lemon juice and extra virgin olive oil together, season with salt and add parsley to make a dressing.

Spoon dressing over the mushrooms and finish with fresh milled black pepper. Serve with extra lemon wedges for taste.

Everyone loves gnocchi. You can also make them with pumpkin. Choose any sauce for gnocchi—let your imagination run wild.

Gnocchi al gorgonzola

Potato dumplings with gorgonzola

Serves 4

500g (1lb) old potatoes
250g (8oz) plain flour
100ml (3fl oz) chicken stock
250ml (8fl oz) fresh cream
100g (3½oz) gorgonzola
50g (2oz) parmesan cheese, grated
Freshly crushed black pepper, to taste

Place whole, unpeeled potatoes in cold water, bring to boil and cook through. Drain and peel the potatoes while still warm.

Mash the potato and add flour. Knead to form an even and smooth consistency. Roll out approximately 100g (3½oz) at a time into thick strips of 1cm (½in) diameter.

Using a scraper or pallet knife, cut into pieces approximately 1cm (½in) in length. Roll each piece into an oval ball and with your forefinger in a downward motion form a concave shape in each one. You can also run a fork over each dumpling to create little ridges.

In a large pot bring to boil approximately 2 litres (3½pints) of salted water. Add gnocchi and stir.

As the gnocchi float to the top, remove from the pan and place into a bowl of iced water to arrest the cooking process, then immediately place in a large container ready to be added to the sauce. In a frying pan, bring the stock, cream and gorgonzola to the boil over a high heat, stirring frequently. Reduce to a thick consistency. Add drained gnocchi and mix well through sauce, toss through the parmesan cheese and sprinkle with pepper. Serve hot.

Unlike potato gnocchi, these are much larger and ideal for the winter months. They are great for a dinner party; they can be prepared ahead, refrigerated and just heated up in the oven when you're ready.

I suggest a young merlot for this dish, and because of the presence of nutmeg, a cabernet, either a straight variety or a blend, would suit it just as well.

Gnocchi verdi

Spinach and ricotta dumplings

Serves 4

For Béchamel Sauce

250ml (8fl oz) milk
25g (1oz) butter
25g (1oz) plain flour, sifted

Bring the milk to the boil and set aside.

In another pot, melt the butter, being careful not to burn it, add the flour slowly and cook for about 1 minute.

Add the milk slowly, stirring continuously, until it's all used, and bring back up to boil. Place aside ready for further use.

100g (3½oz) baby English spinach leaves
200g (61½oz) fresh ricotta
Pinch grated nutmeg
Salt and pepper, to taste
50g (2oz) parmesan, grated

Blanch spinach in boiling salted water, drain.

Chop the spinach finely and mix with the ricotta and nutmeg. Season to taste. Make large dumplings from the mixture. Wet your hands with water and shape a ball by cupping the palm of your hand in a circular motion. Place on buttered serving dishes. Cover with the béchamel sauce and sprinkle with parmesan.

Bake in a pre-heated oven at 180°C (350°F) Gas Mark 4 for approximately 7 to 10 minutes or until desired colour is achieved. Serve with extra grated parmesan cheese and fresh crushed pepper.

This dish can be served as either an entrée or as part of an antipasto platter.The acidity of the lime goes well with an unwooded chardonnay or traminer riesling.

Involtini di asparagi al limo

Prosciutto-wrapped asparagus with lime

Serves 4

3 bunches asparagus (5 spears per serve)
4 slices of prosciutto crudo
Plain flour
Egg wash
Breadcrumbs
Vegetable oil for frying
1 bunch shallots (spring onion, scallions)
30g (1oz) salted butter
80ml (2½fl oz) chicken stock
200ml (6½fl oz) cream
Salt and pepper, to taste
100g (3½oz) mascarpone
2 fresh limes

Trim asparagus to size, approximately 13cm (5in) and cut off any woody ends. Blanch in boiling salted water, cool in iced water then allow to dry.

Wrap asparagus, in bunches of 5, in prosciutto then dip in the flour, egg wash and breadcrumbs.

Heat the oil in a heavy pan until hot. Cook the wrapped asparagus until golden brown on all sides. Remove and drain, season with salt.

Sauté the chopped shallots in a frying pan in butter for a few minutes, add stock and cream and cook to further combine all the flavours, adding a little salt, then the mascarpone. Squeeze the juice of one lime then reduce the sauce over a high heat, stirring frequently, to a thick consistency.

Cut the other lime into wedges for added flavour. Place your asparagus on a serving plate, pour the sauce over, serve with freshly crushed pepper and a wedge of lime.

This dish originated in Positano as a celebration of summer; its rich colours represent freshness and vitality in food. If you can't find squid-infused pasta you can add a little fresh squid ink to the dish while cooking. You could also add a little chilli. A nice bottle of pinot grigio, preferably an Italian one which has a much higher mineral content, would be good with this.

Don't be shy with the salt, you need to drag out the natural flavours. All you should taste are the raw fresh ingredients.

Linguette ai fiori

Squid pasta with zucchini flowers

Serves 4

- 600g (1¼lb) squid ink pasta dried linguette or fettuccine (flat long pasta)
- 3 San Marzano (roma) tomatoes
- 150g (5oz) fresh green prawns (shrimp)
- 150g (2oz) fresh calamari
- Salt, to taste
- 3 cloves fresh garlic, sliced
- 100g (3½oz) small zucchini (courgette)
- 90ml (2½fl oz) dry white wine
- 4 stems continental parsley, chopped
- 80ml (2½fl oz) extra virgin olive oil
- 12 zucchini flowers, roughly torn

Cut all ingredients to desired length and size.

Cook the pasta to *al dente* (firm). Drain but do not rinse it under water, you need the natural starch.

De-seed the tomatoes, keeping only the outside pulp with the skin on.

Place the oil in a heavy frying pan on the stove over a high heat. When the oil is hot, add the prawns and calamari and salt, cook for a few minutes, then add the garlic, zucchini and tomato, also adding a little more salt. Cook for a further 2 minutes. You can add some chillies now if you prefer a slightly hotter dish.

Deglaze the pan with the wine, cook for a further 3 minutes or until all the liquids are hot. Add the pasta to the frying pan, stirring frequently, and sprinkle in parsley, ½ the amount of oil and the zucchini flowers last (otherwise they will turn bitter).

Place on individual large flat plates or a platter, drizzle oil around the plate and serve. And please, under no circumstances is this dish to have parmesan cheese!

Linguette allo zafferano

Pasta with saffron

Serves 4

2 packets (600g, 1¼lb) saffron linguette
¼ white onion, finely diced
Vegetable oil
100g (3½oz) fresh uncooked Lobster or Moreton Bay bug meat, diced
Salt, to taste
Pinch saffron strands
30ml (1fl oz) fish stock
100ml (3fl oz) fresh cream
Fresh crushed pepper, to taste
No cheese please

Cook the linguette in 6 litres (10½ pints) of boiling salted water to *al dente* stage (firm to the tooth), stirring constantly. Set aside to drain.

Meanwhile, sauté the onion in a heavy frying pan with some vegetable oil, add the lobster or bug meat, season lightly with salt and add saffron.

Deglaze the pan with fish stock, reduce the sauce and then add the cream. Reduce further. Add the drained, cooked linguette, mix well and serve with pepper. And please, under no circumstances is this dish to have cheese!

ESSENTIAL TOMATOES:
Il Pomodoro

Il pomodoro (pomo d'oro) simply means the golden apple, a fruit that originated in South America and was eaten by the Incas of Peru. Now it is grown in most countries in the world. It was not until the early 1500s that tomatoes were introduced to the Italians. At first it was regarded as a poor man's food but slowly made its way into the houses of the nobility.

In the early 1700s successful cultivation was achieved and it began to be really popular in the 1800s served with fish and meat and especially as a cooked sauce. Today the tomato is used in almost every cuisine and there is a large variety; from large plump round ones, to egg-shaped romas, to the cherry tomato, all in colours ranging from a deep red to almost lime green.

Generally you can buy tomatoes all year round but the peak of the growing season is the middle of summer. If you treat your tomatoes well you will be rewarded with a superior taste. Never store them in the fridge, keep them in a dark place, away from direct sunlight, to allow them to ripen. Discard fruit that is too soft or bruised as this will affect the rest of the tomatoes and attract fruit flies.

In some parts of Naples during the winter months you can see cherry tomatoes threaded on strings, hung on balconies and left to dry in the sun, ready to be picked as needed. To preserve

tomatoes at home, preheat your oven to very hot then after about 10 minutes turn it off. Cut tomatoes in half and place them on an oven tray. Sprinkle over a generous amount of salt and olive oil and leave the tray of tomatoes in the oven overnight. The next morning, spoon them into a sterilised jar with parsley and whole cloves of garlic and cover with olive oil.

Another popular way to preserve them is in a sauce. In Italy we call this salsa pomodoro.

Salsa pomodoro

Fresh tomato sauce

- 60ml (2fl oz) extra virgin olive oil
- 2 cloves garlic, sliced
- 250g (8 oz) tomatoes, peeled
- Salt, to taste
- 3 stalks basil

In a small pot, heat up the oil over a high heat. Add garlic and tomatoes. Season with salt and cook for 15 minutes then add basil and cook for a further 5 minutes. The noble tomato…a fruit to be celebrated!

Linguette al nero di seppia al tonno

Squid pasta with tuna

Serves 4

2 packets (600g, 1¼lb) squid ink linguette
50ml (2fl oz) olive oil
2 cloves garlic, peeled and sliced
1 small chilli, finely chopped
300g (9½oz) fresh tuna fillet, cut into small cubes
4 large ripe roma tomatoes, cut into cubes of approximately 2cm (¾in)
200g (6½oz) large green olives
Salt and black pepper, to taste
1 small bunch continental parsley, chopped
50ml (2fl oz) extra virgin olive oil
No cheese please

Cook the linguette in 6 litres (10½ pints) of boiling salted water to *al dente* stage (firm to the tooth), stirring constantly.

While the pasta is cooking, heat the olive oil in a large pan over high heat. Add the garlic and chilli and sauté quickly without browning or burning the garlic.

Add the tuna and sauté to sear quickly. Add the tomatoes and olives. Season with salt.

Continue to cook until the tomatoes are soft and a sauce is created in the pan. Add the drained pasta and the parsley, pour over the extra virgin olive oil and toss through. Serve on plates, finishing with black pepper.

Linguette di spinaci al formaggio e noci

Spinach pasta with walnuts and cheese

Serves 4

100g (3½oz) gorgonzola
200ml (6½fl oz) thickened cream
100ml (3fl oz) stock (chicken or vegetable)
2 packets (600g, 1¼lb) of spinach linguette
100g (3½oz) walnuts, chopped
50g (2oz) parmesan
Pepper, to taste

In a shallow frying pan, bring the gorgonzola, cream and stock to a light simmer. Reduce by half.

Cook the linguette in 6 litres (10½ pints) of boiling salted water to *al dente* stage (firm), stirring constantly.

Place the strained pasta in a large bowl. Sprinkle over it the walnuts and parmesan and add the sauce.

Serve with fresh crushed pepper.

On any Sunday morning in Naples you can smell the aroma of onions cooking in olive oil with a mixture of beef, pork, peeled tomato and good red wine. This is the ritual of almost every Neapolitan household and has been so for hundreds of years. Ragu recipes have been passed down through generations. It takes 2 to 3 hours to cook and works up the biggest appetite, a bit like the smell of onions on a barbecue. Ragu is served over a range of short pasta or even gnocchi.

Ragu

Bolognese sauce

Serves 6

- 100ml (3fl oz) olive oil
- 2 onions, diced
- 150g (5oz) chuck steak, diced
- 150g (5oz) neck or shoulder pork, diced
- Salt and pepper, to taste
- 100ml (3fl oz) red wine (sangiovese)
- 50g (2oz) triple concentrated tomato paste
- 2 bay leaves
- 2 cloves
- 500g (1lb) Italian peeled tomato
- 900g (2lb) rigatoni
- 120g grated parmesan cheese

In a pot, heat the oil and sauté the onion for 10 minutes, add the meat, season, and reduce the juices making sure that you stir frequently.

Add the wine and allow to evaporate and reduce.

Mix in the tomato paste well, add the cloves and bay leaf and the tomatoes. Season again.

Turn the heat down to a very low simmer and allow cooking for 2 to 3 hours, stirring to make sure that it will not stick to the pot.

Cook the rigatoni in salted water. Drain and place in a bowl. Add the ragu with a generous amount of parmesan cheese.

In restaurants we try and use all the off cuts and often get some amazing results from them, so for this dish you can use the remainder of the meat on the duck after you have removed the breasts for Anatra al Forno (see page 111).

The best wine for both cooking and drinking with this dish is a shiraz. Don't forget to stir—a good meal takes time and passion.

Ragu di anatra

Duck bolognese

Serves 4

- 100ml (3fl oz) olive oil
- 100g (4oz) onion, chopped
- 50g (2oz) pancetta, diced small, skin off but fat on
- 300g (10oz) duck meat, diced small, trimmed of all fat
- Salt, to taste
- 200ml (6fl oz) shiraz
- 100g (3½oz) tomato paste
- 3 whole bay leaves
- 2 whole cloves
- 400g (13oz) whole peeled tomatoes passed through a moulinex
- 600g (1¼lb) fusilli (spiral pasta)
- Parmesan, grated

Over a high heat and in a heavy, deep pot, heat olive oil, add onion and sauté until it becomes a translucent colour.

Add pancetta and sauté to release fat and flavour, then the duck meat and seasoning. Cook until all liquid has reduced and meat begins to fry.

Pour in the red wine and, stirring constantly, reduce to almost nothing.

Add the tomato paste, bay leaves, cloves. When all the tomato has coated the meat add the peeled tomatoes, season with salt and bring to the boil over a high heat. Reduce the heat to simmer and allow to cook, stirring occasionally for 2–3 hours.

Half way through the cooking, correct the seasoning to desired taste. Cook pasta in boiling salted water to *al dente* stage (firm).

Stir the ragu through the pasta in a large pan and serve in bowls, finishing with fresh parmesan.

Use fresh porcini if you can but otherwise the dried ones are fine. This particular dish needs your full attention, stirring frequently for at least 15 to 20 minutes.

I would drink a pinot noir, a light burgundy style of wine or even a chianti as long as it's not cheap and nasty.

Risotto ai funghi porcini

Risotto with porcini mushrooms

Serves 4

- 200g (6½oz) dried porcini mushrooms
- Olive oil
- 100g (3½oz) white onions, finely diced
- 200g (6½oz) arborio rice
- 1 litre (1¾pints) chicken stock
- Butter, knob
- 50g (2oz) parmesan, grated
- Pepper, to taste

Soak the porcini mushrooms for a couple of hours or overnight in warm water.

Place a little oil in a deep large frying pan and cook the onions till soft and golden colour.

Add the raw rice and stir frequently.

Bring the stock to the boil.

After approximately 5 minutes, when you notice the rice turning a translucent colour, add the drained porcini.

Make sure the stock is boiling, then add one ladle at a time, and as it reduces add some more, until the rice is cooked and all the flavours are incorporated into this dish.

When the rice is almost cooked add a good knob of butter, stir through.

Place on a serving plate, add parmesan and some freshly crushed pepper, serve immediately.

Even though this recipe looks difficult and time consuming, it's quite the opposite. It's perfect served cold as an entrée, lunch or brunch along with a sparkling white.

Salmone Atlantico all erbette

Cured Atlantic salmon

Serves 4

1 large fillet of fresh salmon
400g (13oz) sugar and salt
2 bunch chives, chopped
50g (2oz) crushed black pepper
1 lemon, juiced
Seeded mustard
Salsa mayonnaise (see page 104)
50g (2oz) capers
Extra virgin olive oil

Ask your fish supplier to give you a side of salmon that is totally free of bones with the skin on. Place it on perforated tray to drain juices, coat with even amount of salt and sugar (this is the curing process). Place a tray on top with a heavy weight, and leave in the refrigerator for one day. The following day remove the excess sugar and salt (run your hands under running water to take any residual salt or sugar off). Pat dry with kitchen towel.

Mix 1 bunch of the chives with crushed pepper then evenly coat the whole salmon, still keeping it skin side down, wrap in cling wrap and place in the fridge for 2 hours. This allows some of the flavours to take.

Slice thinly, not cutting into the skin, leave that on purely as a guide. Arrange the thin, flat slices on a serving dish, add lemon juice, a little mustard, mayonnaise, chives and capers.

Drizzle a little extra virgin olive oil and serve with crostini (little pieces of toast).

Fresh sardines are seasonal, a very high source of omega-3 fatty acids and are readily found in our local fish markets or seafood suppliers. They are plentiful off the coast of Sardinia (that's where the name comes from). Always use the fresh fish. Fried, baked or grilled they are great with a glass of cold beer.

Sardine indorate e' fritte

Fried sardines

Serves 4

- 4 large eggs
- ½ bunch continental parsley, chopped
- 40g (1½oz) grated parmesan cheese
- Vegetable oil
- 20 fresh sardines, filleted
- Flour
- 1 bunch curly endive
- 2 lemons

In a bowl whisk the eggs, parley and cheese.

Place the oil in a shallow frying pan on the stove and bring the heat up for frying.

Coat your sardines in the flour and shake off any excess.

Dip them in the egg wash and slowly place them in the hot oil and fry to a golden colour.

Place on a paper towel to drain the excess oil and season with salt. Arrange the white part of the curly endive on a plate, place your sardines on top and squeeze the lemon over and serve.

This is not a risotto, it's more of a pilaf—a very filling entrée. A straight merlot will go well with this dish.

Sartu' di riso

Rice terrine

Serves 4

- 600ml (20fl oz) chicken stock, seasoned
- 300g (9½oz) short grain rice of good quality
- 1 onion, diced very small
- 50g (2oz) butter
- 50g (2oz) fresh or frozen peas
- 50g (2oz) chicken livers
- 50g (2oz) salami, diced
- 100g (3½oz) smoked provola or bocconcini cheese, diced
- 2 hard boiled eggs, diced
- 200g (6½oz) ragu (see page 89)
- 50g (2oz) grana padano parmesan cheese
- 50g (2oz) breadcrumbs
- Salt and pepper to taste
- 40ml (1½fl oz) olive oil

Bring the stock to the boil.

Add the unwashed rice, stirring constantly, turn the heat to simmer and cook until *al dente* (firm).

Fry the onion with oil and butter in a frying pan, stirring frequently. Add the peas and cook for 5 minutes, reducing any juices, then add the chicken livers and cook for a further 15 minutes on medium heat.

In a bowl mix the drained rice, peas, chicken livers, salami, provola or bocconcini, eggs, half the ragu and parmesan cheese.

Coat an oven dish not higher then 2cm (¾in) with butter and half the breadcrumbs, then put in the rice and sprinkle the rest of the breadcrumbs evenly over the dish.

Place in a pre-heated oven, 180°C (350°F) Gas Mark 4, and allow to bake for 20 minutes.

Leave to rest for 5 minutes, turn upside down on to a serving dish, finish it with remaining ragu, and sprinkle parmesan cheese on top. Finish the dish with a good drizzle of extra virgin olive oil.

This twist on traditional pesto is an extremely tasty entrée. Serve with a good wooded chardonnay and try not to follow this dish with seafood.

Spaghetti al pesto rozzo

Spaghetti with rough cut pesto

Serves 6

- 100ml (3fl oz) extra virgin olive oil
- 2 garlic cloves, whole
- 250g (8oz) macadamia nuts, chopped
- 100g (3½oz) slow roasted tomato
- ½ bunch basil, chopped
- 50g (2oz) parmesan cheese, grated
- 500g (1lb) spaghetti
- Parmesan cheese, shaved

Heat the oil in a large frying pan, and sauté the garlic until a golden colour, remove from the pan and discard. You may leave the garlic in for added flavour if you wish.

Add the macadamias to the pan and stir frequently whilst cooking. Now mix in the tomatoes, basil and grated parmesan.

Cook your pasta *al dente*, (firm) add a spoonful of water from the pasta to the frying pan and stir.

When pasta is ready drain and add to the pan, tossing to make sure that it is evenly coated with all the ingredients.

Place on a serving plate and sprinkle with shaved parmesan and pepper.

Vitello tonnato is a classic dish that originated in Piedmont in the north of Italy in the early 1800s. You will find this dish served in almost every Italian eatery in the world and just as many recipes have been written for it. This is my recipe, I adore it and eat it regularly. Generally it's served as an antipasto, but my preference is to serve it as an entrée with some crusty Italian bread. It can all be prepared a day in advance, leaving you with more time to enjoy a glass of wine with your guests. A glass of sparkling white or a young vibrant pinot grigio suits it quite well.

Vitello tonnato

Braised veal and tuna mayonnaise

Serves 4

2 teaspoons vegetable oil
500g (1lb) veal back strap, trimmed of all fat
2 stalks celery, diced
1 stalks leek, diced
2 carrots, diced
2 bay leaves
Salt and pepper, to taste
100ml (3fl oz) white wine
1 litre (1¾pints) veal stock
6 whole black peppercorns
Salsa Tonnato (see page 104)

Heat oil in oven tray. Season the meat evenly and seal on all sides. Remove it from the tray and leave in a warm place to rest. In the same tray drizzle in a touch more oil and place the celery, leek, carrots, bay leaves and seasoning, stir whilst cooking for 5 minutes.

Return the meat to the tray, deglaze the pan with the wine, then add enough veal stock to cover the meat and sprinkle over the whole peppercorns.

Bring to the boil then reduce to simmer and cook meat to medium rare, approximately 15 minutes.

Remove the meat and strain the cooking liquid over it, allow to cool then place in the fridge covered with cling wrap.

To serve, slice the cooled meat thinly with, if possible, a slicing machine. Arrange meat on the serving plate ready for the sauce.

Salsa mayonnaise

2 large egg yolks
50ml (2 fl oz) white vinegar
250ml (8fl oz) vegetable oil
Hot water
Salt, to taste
1 lemon, juiced

In a blender or food processor add yolks and vinegar. Blend adding the vegetable oil slowly until combined. Hot water can be added to whiten mayonnaise and help combine all ingredients. Season with salt to taste and finish with the lemon juice.

Salsa tonnato

Salsa mayonnaise
50g (2oz) tinned tuna
3 anchovy fillets
20g (½oz) capers
3 gherkins

Blend salsa mayonnaise with all other ingredients in a blender or food processor to the required consistency. Mix the ingredients through mayonnaise. Spread the sauce thinly over sliced meat and garnish with gherkins or capers.

Right: *My other passion is cars.*

Macaroni and cheese is generally a dish that kids love, so I guess I am very much a kid at heart because I adore this dish. Choose any four cheeses you like but these are my favourites and they work well.

Maccheroni ai quattro formaggi

Pasta with four cheeses

Serves 4

600g (1¼lb) rigatoni
100ml (3fl oz) cream
100ml (3fl oz) chicken stock
50g (2oz) fontina, chopped
50g (2oz) mozzarella, chopped
50g (2oz) grana padano, chopped
30g (1oz) mascarpone
Parmesan, grated
Freshly crushed pepper, to taste

Cook the rigatoni in 6 litres (10½ pints) of boiling salted water to *al dente* stage (firm to the tooth), stirring constantly.

Place a frying pan over a high heat and add the cream and stock. Bring to the boil and then reduce.

Add the cheeses, stirring well and being careful not to let the sauce stick to the pan.

Add the cooked strained pasta, tossing the pan to make sure that an even coating is achieved.

Pour the pasta in an oven-proof platter or individual plate, sprinkle some parmesan cheese over it, then place in a pre-heated moderate oven, 180°C (350°F) Gas Mark 4 and bake until slightly brown or caramelised on top of the dish.

Without removing from its dish serve with freshly crushed or milled pepper

When winter is upon us and the mercury is falling you need good comfort food like lentil soup. This soup is very high in iron, antioxidants and vitamins. However, it also contains saturated fat because in a cold climate fat is an important component of the winter diet.

Minestra di lenticchie

Lentil soup

Serves 4

- 60ml (2fl oz) olive oil
- 3 medium carrots
- 1 large leek
- ½ bunch small celery
- 4 slices flat pancetta (with fat on)
- 3 bay leaves
- Salt, to taste
- 4 litres (7 pints) water
- 200g (6½oz) brown lentils
- 3 tomatoes, de-seeded and chopped
- ½ bunch continental parsley, chopped
- 50g (2oz) parmesan cheese, grated
- 60ml (2fl oz) extra virgin olive oil
- Pepper, to taste

Chop all the ingredients into small pieces.

In a heavy pot (or even a terracotta one) heat the olive oil and sauté the carrots, leek, celery and pancetta, together with the bay leaves for about 5 minutes stirring frequently over a moderate to high heat and don't forget to salt liberally.

Add the water and lentils at the same time and bring to the boil. After which turn the heat down to low for simmering.

Simmer for about 1 hour and then add the tomatoes, cooking for a further 30 minutes.

Place in a soup bowl, adding the parsley, parmesan and drizzle with the extra virgin olive oil. Add pepper to taste.

When served to your guests, prepare chargrilled crusty bread as an accompaniment.

Mains

Mains

This dish is all about marinated meat. Rabbit, wild boar or pheasant could also be used. You can substitute white wine in this dish depending on the meat you have chosen.

Anatra al forno

Braised duck breast

Serves 4

- 4 duck breasts
- 1 onion, chopped
- 2 carrots, chopped
- 2 stalks of celery, chopped
- 1 orange, sliced
- 12 juniper berries, crushed
- 3 bay leaves
- 1 bottle red wine (preferably sangiovese)
- 8 baby onions
- Rock salt
- Oil

Place the duck in a shallow container with the onion, carrots, celery, orange, juniper berries and bay leaves, then totally cover this with red wine (one that you would drink with the meal). Cover and leave to marinate in the fridge for a minimum of 5 hours, even overnight. Without taking the skin off the baby onions place them in a baking dish, cover with some rock salt and oil and cook in a moderate oven, 180°C (350°F) Gas Mark 4 for at least 1 hour or until they are caramelised.Take the duck out of the marinade, pat dry, season liberally with salt and start to sear, skin side down, then place in pre-heated moderate oven, 180°C (350°F) Gas Mark 4 for approximately 15 minutes.

Whilst cooking the duck, place the marinade in a pot over a high heat and start reducing. When the marinade comes to the boil, strain then reduce further to a thick consistency.

When the duck is cooked, leave it in a warm place to rest.

Slice the duck and place on a plate, serve with the peeled roasted onions, cover with wine reduction and if you wish a nice dollop of mash potato, or a simple basil and pine nuts risotto as accompaniment.

This is my version of a classic dish that has been eaten by my family for generations. About halfway through cooking this, when the tomato is warm but not yet cooked, slice some crusty Italian bread, dip it in the sauce and taste it; this is my way of testing for the seasoning of the dish. A cool climate pinot noir goes with this dish like two lovers in lust.

Braciolette di vitello

Baby veal filled with pinenuts

Serves 4

- 600g (1lb3½oz) veal back strap
- 40g (1½oz) sultanas
- 40g (1½oz) pine nuts
- 40g (1½oz) continental parsley, chopped
- 1 egg
- 20g (¾oz) grana padano parmesan cheese
- 20g (¾oz) breadcrumbs
- 1 onion, finely chopped
- Salt and pepper, pinch
- 100ml (3fl oz) olive oil
- 1 onion, diced
- Flour for coating
- 100ml (3fl oz) red wine (pinot noir)
- 250g (8oz) peeled tomatoes
- Rocket
- Red wine vinegar
- Extra virgin olive oil

Slice veal on a slight angle, into 12 slices. Flatten or tenderise with a mallet.

Mix together sultana, pine nuts, parsley, egg, parmesan, breadcrumbs, onion, salt and pepper.

Lay out the meat and divide the filling evenly on each piece, roll up and hold with toothpicks.

Heat the olive oil in a large frying pan or a flat roasting tray. Sauté diced onion. Coat the meat in flour and sear on all sides.

Deglaze the pan with red wine and reduce over a high heat, stirring frequently. Add the tomatoes, season with salt and bring to boil, then reduce the heat to a simmer.

Cook for 20 minutes, stirring frequently, so it doesn't stick to the bottom. Remove meat and toothpicks from the pan, continue to reduce the sauce. Place sauce on serving plate and arrange meat on top.

Garnish plate with fresh rocket, dressed with red wine vinegar, salt and extra virgin olive oil.

Use spring lamb in this dish because it doesn't need camouflaging with heavy sauces. The smell you are going for is of rich, black, wet soil on a rainy day. Do not substitute dried herbs. A light chianti wine is the perfect match to this delicate dish.

Agnello primavera

Spring lamb with artichokes

Serves 4

- 3 large fresh artichokes or roasted roman tinned artichokes in oil
- Flour, pinch
- 1 lemon, cut into wedges
- 10g (½oz) fresh rosemary, very finely chopped
- 10g (½oz) fresh thyme, very finely chopped
- 10g (½oz) fresh sage, very finely chopped
- 3 cloves of garlic, finely chopped
- 60ml (2fl oz) extra virgin olive oil
- Salt and pepper, to taste
- 800g (1lb 9½oz) rack of lamb (each rack should be 4 bones)
- Oil, for frying
- 100g (3½oz) pine nuts
- 30g (1oz) crepinette (caul fat)

Peel the artichokes, and place in water with a pinch of flour and wedges of lemon to stop them from turning brown. Leave for 15 minutes, then cut the artichoke in quarters, discard the frilly part and wash with fresh water, then dry with towel, coat them very lightly with oil and grill over volcanic rocks or charcoal. You can also poach them for 10 minutes before grilling.

Finely chop the artichokes, combine with the garlic and herbs in a bowl, add half of the oil then season.

Coat the lamb with the herbs and garlic. Coat the lamb with half the amount of artichokes. Wrap each rack with the caul fat.

Heat up some oil in a frying pan, sear the rack and season with salt, then place it in the oven for 15 minutes. Cook to medium rare (180°, 350°F, Gas Mark 4).

Leave the meat in a warm place to rest.

Place the pan that was previously used to cook the lamb over a high heat, add the remaining artichokes and cook for 5 minutes.

Cut the racks, arrange on a large flat plate or platter spoon the remaining artichokes on top, drizzle the remainder of oil around the dish and serve immediately.

Agnello all' insalata

Lamb salad

Serves 4

- 100ml (3fl oz) sesame seed oil
- 2 cloves garlic, chopped
- 400g (13oz) lamb loin, seasoned
- 100ml (3fl oz) lamb or veal stock
- Salt and pepper, to taste
- 20ml (½fl oz) sherry vinegar
- Mixed lettuce
- 50g (2oz) sesame seeds

In a heavy frying pan, heat the oil (leave a tablespoon aside) and sauté your garlic. Add lamb and seal on all side. Place in a preheated oven (180°, 350°F, Gas Mark 4) for 10 minutes until rare. Remove from oven and leave in a warm place to rest.

Deglaze pan with stock and vinegar and leave to a slow simmer.

Place the mixed lettuce in a bowl and season, adding a tablespoon of sesame oil.

Transfer to a serving dish, slice the lamb, placing it on the lettuce, sprinkle with the sesame seeds and pepper and pour the liquid from the pan over the salad and serve hot or warm.

The secret to this dish is simplicity. A dry aged riesling is a perfect companion to this dish.

Costatelle di vitello al forno

Roasted veal

Serves 4

- 200g (6½oz) cocktail onions, peeled and quartered
- 100g (3½oz) oven roasted tomatoes
- Salt and pepper, to taste
- 1kg (2lb) veal racks
- 50ml (1½fl oz) olive oil
- 3 stems of fresh marjoram
- 50ml (1½fl oz) extra virgin olive oil

Keeping the skin on, pre-roast your onions in a very slow oven, 50°C (100°F) Gas Mark ½ for 1 hour. Cut the tomatoes into quarters and don't disturb them when they are cooking in the same oven for about ½ an hour.

Before adding the onions to the meat, peel away the first 2 layers and add whole. Cut the veal racks into 4 portions, allowing 4 bones per serve.

In frying pan heat oil, then sear the veal racks on both sides. Add the onions, tomatoes and marjoram and season with salt and pepper. Place in a moderately hot oven, 200°C (400°F) Gas Mark 5 for 15 minutes. Remove the pan from the oven and leave to rest for 5 minutes.

Remove the veal and place on serving dish.

Place the remaining ingredients over the veal with a sprig of marjoram; lightly drizzle with extra virgin olive oil. Serve with fresh spring vegetables.

This dish won first place in the Queensland Signature Dish Competition. It was created by one of my business partners, Australian chef Richard Burt who now runs the Fellini kitchen with my sister Anna. It's a difficult dish to make, but take the time and your guests will be blown away.

Cinghiale alle pere

Wild boar with prosciutto-wrapped pear

Serves 4

- 2 x 8-bone wild boar racks
- 4 semi-ripe pears
- 4 thin slices prosciutto
- 30ml (1fl oz) olive oil
- Salt and black pepper, to taste
- 60ml (2fl oz) verjuice
- 100ml (3fl oz) veal stock
- 30ml (1fl oz) extra virgin olive oil
- Chives for garnish

Cut each rack in half, allowing 4 ribs per portion. Cut pear in half horizontally, then peel the top half, leaving the stem attached. Wrap the top half with a slice of prosciutto.

Cut bottom half of pears into quarters removing centre core and seeds. In heavy ovenproof pan, heat olive oil and seal wild boar racks on all sides. Season with salt and pepper. Place pan into moderate oven, 180°C (350°F) Gas Mark 4, for 15 minutes.

Remove pan and spoon off excess fat, turn boar racks over and place wrapped and quartered pears into pan, deglaze pan with verjuice and add 1/3 of veal stock. Return pan to the oven for 10 minutes. Remove pan from oven, remove boar racks from pan and allow to rest for 5 minutes in warm place. While boar is resting, place wrapped pear, off centre on the serving plate. Add remaining veal stock to the pan and reduce to a thick consistency.

Remove the quartered pears from the pan and slice in half, arrange pieces in the middle of serving plate alongside the wrapped pear. Cut the boar racks into cutlets and arrange on top of the sliced pear and around the wrapped pear. Spoon the reduced glaze over the meat and drizzle the plate with a fine line of extra virgin olive oil. Garnish with stems of chives; finish with fresh cracked black pepper.

CHASSEUR

I use farmed white rabbit meat as it is much more tender than wild game.

Coniglio alla cacciatore

Rabbit casserole

Serves 4

- 1 whole rabbit, cut into pieces
- 500ml (16fl oz) dry white wine, for marinade
- 500ml (16fl oz) white vine vinegar
- 100ml (3fl oz) extra virgin olive oil
- 4 cloves of garlic
- 3 whole chillies
- 150ml (5fl oz) good dry white wine
- 300g (9½oz) peeled tomatoes, squashed
- Salt and pepper, to taste

Place the rabbit in a dish and cover with the wine and vinegar. Cover and place in the fridge overnight.

In a large heavy casserole dish, heat up the oil, sauté the garlic and chillies, add the rabbit and cook for 10 minutes, stirring frequently.

Deglaze the dish with the wine, allowing most of the juice to evaporate over a high heat.

Add the tomatoes, season, turn the heat to low, cover the pot and cook for 2 hours, or till tender. If the sauce dries out too quickly add some water.

Serve in a deep dish with crusty Italian bread.

As you open up the paper packaging in front of your guests, the aroma from this dish will send them into a culinary trance! Soave classico will not camouflage the sweetness of the zucchini and onion.

Dentice in cartoccio

Wrapped baked snapper

Serves 4

- 60ml (2fl oz) olive oil
- 600g (1¼lb) snapper fillet
- Salt, to taste
- 100g (3½oz) zucchini (courgette), sliced
- 1 bunch shallots (spring onion, scallions), chopped
- 100g (3½oz) oven roasted tomatoes
- Fresh thyme
- 100ml (3fl oz) white wine
- 60ml (2fl oz) fish stock
- Oven-proof or parchment paper, torn into individual pieces
- 60ml (2fl oz) extra virgin olive oil

Heat the oil in a pan, season the snapper with salt and sear on both sides.

Take your fish out of the pan and keep in a warm place to rest while you add the zucchini, shallots and tomatoes and cook for 5 minutes over a high heat.

Return the fish to the pan, add thyme, then deglaze the pan with first the wine then the stock. Keep the heat on high and when hot transfer the fish with all the ingredients, including the juices, into the individual paper, closing all the sides up, so no steam can escape.

Pre-heat the oven to moderately hot, 200 °C (400F) Gas Mark 5. Place your envelopes in the oven and bake for 5 minutes.

Cut a slit in the paper, drizzle with extra virgin olive oil and serve.

There's always going to be one dinner party when you want to impress your guests. Well, this is a dish that is not easy to cook, but the rewards are enormous. The best wine for this is a straight merlot—choose one that has a bit of age, at least 10 years.

Your pheasant has to be fresh, not frozen—you will taste the difference and so will your guests. You can make the demiglasse the day before. Once made, cool it on the kitchen bench before placing it in the refrigerator. Don't walk away from this dish when cooking, it requires some tender loving care.

Fagiano alle pere renette tartufato

Pheasant with pears and risotto

Serves 4

Stock

- 2 pheasants
- 1 carrot, roughly chopped
- 1 stalk celery, roughly chopped
- 1 onion, roughly chopped
- 2 stems fresh sage
- 100ml (3fl oz) merlot

Make the stock: Remove breast from pheasant, (or ask your butcher to portion for you) and set aside.

Brown pheasant bones and legs in deep pan with a small amount of oil. Add vegetables and 2 sage stems, brown evenly.

Deglaze pot with merlot, reduce liquid till almost dry.

Add enough water to cover the bones, bring to the boil, and reduce heat and simmer for approximately 3 hours. Strain through a fine sieve and cook for a further 1 hour. Reserve for later use.

Risotto

20g (¾oz) dried porcini mushrooms
Olive oil
40g (1½oz) onions, finely diced
100g (3½oz) arborio rice
100ml (3fl oz) white wine
Salt, to taste
Stock (see previous page)

Make the risotto: Soak mushrooms for 15 minutes in warm water. Heat oil in heavy frying pan, add onion, fry till a light golden, translucent colour. Strain porcini and finely dice. Add to pan with rice, stir continuously over a moderate to high heat till coated with the oil.

Add the white wine, season with a little salt, and with a medium size ladle, add the stock (making sure its very hot) one ladle at a time till it is all soaked up by the rice and the rice is cooked *al dente* (firm).

Make sure that you are constantly stirring the rice, it cannot be left unattended.

Pheasant

- 2 pheasant breasts
- Salt and pepper, to taste
- Olive oil
- 4 sage stems
- Stock (see page 124)
- 4 baby green pears
- 4 thin slices prosciutto crudo
- Truffle infused extra virgin olive oil
- Extra virgin olive oil

Season the pheasant breast, then heat oil in a large heavy frying pan and cook it skinside down, then seal both sides.

Place skinside down in a pre-heated oven, 200°C (400°F) Gas Mark 5 for 10 minutes. Remove breast from pan and place in a warm place to rest.

Place the pan over a low heat, add 1 sage stem to the pan and deglaze with stock, reducing the liquid by half.

Return breast to pan, add a small amount of truffle oil to the sauce and reduce until thick.

Place pears on chargrill and sear. Wrap each pear with a slice of prosciutto.

Shred leaves of 2 stems of sage (chiffonade).

To Serve

Place risotto on plate and place the pear next to it. Slice the pheasant on an acute angle, place over the risotto, then pour the sauce around and over the pheasant. Garnish with a sprig and chiffonnade of sage. Pour a thin line of truffle and extra virgin olive oil over the sauce and serve with freshly crushed black pepper.

Variations

If you find fresh truffles, then shave these over the dish just before you serve it, replacing the truffle infused oil. You can marinate the pheasant in red wine with carrot, celery, onion and sage overnight in the fridge. Remove and pat it dry then follow the recipe as before. The strained marinade can be used in your demiglasse, but allow a further 30 minutes of cooking to reduce the alcohol.

The Italian name for this recipe does not mean you have to drive the prawns round in a big car! Limo just means lime, which helps to make this dish so crisp and refreshing. It's designed for a leisurely barbecue and when you can cook the capsicums and put them aside to marinate while you taste another dish.

A very young sauvignon blanc is good with this dish.

Gamberoni al limo

Prawns with lime

Serves 4

- 1 yellow and 2 red capsicums (peppers). This colour distinction is just for visual effect.
- 60ml (2fl oz) extra virgin olive oil
- 3 clove garlic, sliced
- 20 raw king prawns (shrimps)
- 3 limes
- ½ bunch of basil leaves, chopped
- Freshly crushed pepper, to taste

Place the capsicums on a barbecue or open gas flame of the stove and burn the skins until they are black.

While still hot, peel the skin, cut out the membrane, remove seeds and cut into thick strips. You can also allow the capsicum to cool in a plastic bag where it will sweat and the skin will come off more easily. Under no circumstances should you put capsicums under running water—they will lose all their flavour.

Slice the capsicums into quarters and take out seeds. Marinate the pieces in oil and garlic at least 15 minutes prior to serving them.

Skewer the prawns and barbecue them, making sure not to overcook.

Once cooked, arrange on a serving plate, top with the capsicums and marinade, then squeeze the limes over and finish with basil and pepper.

Serve with a fresh garden salad.

Involtini di pollo

Stuffed chicken breast

Serves 4

4 chicken breasts
2 bunches of baby spinach leaves
80g (3oz) mozzarella cheese
80g (3oz) oven or sun dried tomatoes
Flour to dredge
30ml (1fl oz) oil
Salt and pepper, to taste
2 diced freh tomatoes
100ml (3fl oz) chicken stock
¼ bunch fresh basil

Place each chicken breast between 2 sheets of parchment paper, and pound it with a meat cleaver to flatten.

Line the chicken breasts with the spinach, mozzarella and dried tomatoes, season the inside, then roll up and fasten with toothpick.

Dredge in flour and then sauté in a little oil, cooking on all sides. Keeping the chicken in the pan, add the diced tomato and shake the pan for around two minutes while they cook.

Deglaze the pan with the chicken stock, cover and cook for 15 minutes, adding the chopped basil last. Remove the chicken onto a plate and keep warm. Reduce the sauce until it thickens and pour over the chicken.

This dish is best served with either mashed potato or plain wild rice.

When my brother Armando first opened his restaurant with my father Mario, we had just arrived in Australia from Italy. In the 1970s people screwed up their faces at the thought of eating something like octopus, tripe, white bait or livers. But they are a delicacy in Italy, especially in the southern parts. I like to simply cut octopus into small pieces, add the juice of a lemon, some parsley, extra virgin olive oil and pepper, let them sit in the fridge for an hour, then eat them raw with some bread and a glass of dry white wine.

Polpi affogati

Octopus casserole

Serves 4

- 60ml (2fl oz) extra virgin olive oil
- 1 small onion, diced
- 2 bay leaves
- 400g (13oz) vine ripened tomatoes, chopped
- 500g (1lb) medium sized octopus, cleaned, skin on
- 150ml (5fl oz) dry white wine
- 200g (6½oz) fresh peas

In a casserole, heat your oil and sauté the diced onion, and bay leaves add the chopped tomato and cook for 5 minutes, over a moderate heat.

Now, over a high heat, add the octopus one at the time, so the tentacles curl up and soak up the sauce that is gently cooking away. Cook for 5 minutes.

Turn the heat back down to medium, add the wine, cook for 5 minutes then add the peas and cook for another 10 minutes, stirring with a wooden spoon.

Serve in a deep dish, with grilled crusty Italian bread, a drizzle of extra virgin olive oil and pepper.

Note

To clean the octopus take the eyes out, mouth and clean the head part, or ask your fishmonger to do it.

Maiale in padella

Pork loin and peppers

Serves 4

- 8 pork loin chops
- Extra virgin olive oil
- Sprig rosemary
- 3 garlic cloves, sliced
- 1 red and 1 green capsicums (peppers)
- Oil
- Salt and pepper, to taste
- 150ml (5oz) red wine vinegar
- 150ml (5oz) white wine

Marinate pork chops in the oil, rosemary and garlic for at least 2 hours in the fridge, covered in cling film.

Grill the capsicum, then remove the skin, take out the inside membrane and seeds, cut into slices.

Heat some oil in a frying pan, sear the meat on both sides then place in a pre-heated oven for 15 minutes at 220°C (450°F, Gas Mark 6).

Take the pork out of the pan and leave in a warm place. Discard any oil from the pan, add the capsicum, season and cook for 2 minutes. Add the vinegar and white wine, cook for a further 5 minutes, return the pork to the pan, turning to amalgamate flavours.

Place your pork on the plates, reduce the sauce over a high heat, then pour over the pork and serve.

Balsamic vinegar

Like Armani or Cartier, balsamic vinegar is one of the most imitated products in the world today. The real thing is not easy to find so always check the label. Only two places in Italy make true balsamic, Modena and Reggio Emilia. It is dark brown in colour with a slightly richer consistency than normal vinegar and has an intense, complex perfume and a unique taste with a beautiful aromatic acidity.

For centuries balsamic vinegar was highly prized by the nobility for its healing power and antiseptic qualities. The word 'balsam' means something that heals, soothes, or restores. Lucrezia Borgia used it for labour pains, while Francesco IV Duke of Modena would always have a couple of bottles with him to relieve the pain of his ulcers. It was also thought to ward off the plague.

Balsamic vinegar is expensive because the process of making it is long, tiring and leaves no room for mistakes. It all starts with the crushing of the grapes to obtain the 'must'. This is the freshly pressed fruit juice that contains various quantities of pulp such as skins, stems, and seeds.

The must is concentrated over an open flame; reducing its volume by half. It's then poured into wooden barrels and left to rest over the winter months, preferably in an attic for the ideal temperature.

In spring, the process of storing the liquid into different barrels over many years begins. As the liquid gradually evaporates it is poured into smaller and smaller barrels. Each barrel can be made of a different resinous wood which imparts its own special flavour to the vinegar, for example juniper barrels are said to add incredible aromatic qualities.

Choosing the right wood for a barrel is a secret art amongst vinegar makers. The vinegar is stored for between 6 to 12 years until it is ready for the official tasters. They will define the attributes of the DOC (the denomination of origin control) or the DOCG (the denomination of origin control guarantee)

The commercial value of balsamic vinegar is between A$40 to $300 dollars a bottle in the case of *extra vecchio* (extra old). This is because from 350kg (750lb) of grapes you obtain approximately 300 litres (525 pints) of must. After cooking the volume reduces to 100 litres (175 pints) and this is again reduced during storage to approximately 15 litres (27 pints).

It is said that one taste of a truly fine balsamic will make it clear why it is worth all the effort and expense.

Tony Percuoco

This dish is great for lunch or brunch and you can cook it for either two or 20 people. With a chilled rose wine and some crusty bread, you could almost say that this is the perfect dish for the start of a diet!

Pollo all'insalata

Chicken salad

Serves 4

Olive oil
2 Spanish onions, sliced
50g (2oz) pine nuts
400g (13oz) breast of chicken, skin off and cut into strips
Salt and pepper, to taste
60ml (2fl oz) of chicken stock
60ml (2fl oz) balsamic vinegar
Mesculin or mixed lettuce

Heat the oil in a shallow pan, add the sliced onions, season and then sauté for a few minutes.

Add the pine nuts, stir frequently without toasting them, then add the strips of chicken, salt, pepper and cook till golden brown.

Deglaze the pan with the stock, keep the heat on high and lastly add the balsamic vinegar. Reduce all the juices and toss the pan to amalgamate all the flavours.

Place the lettuce on a plate and top with the chicken pieces then evenly spread the rest of the ingredients over the top. Don't forget to include the cooking juices in the dish, you can mop them up with bread. Finish with a generous amount of freshly crushed pepper and WOW!

This dish has been served in our family's restaurants for over 30 years and is almost impossible to take off the menu because everyone knows it. There is no secret to it—just use a very heavy weight while frying.

Galletto alla diavola

Devilled spatchcock

Serves 4

- 4 whole spatchcock (poussin, baby chicken 400g each)
- 2 bay leaves
- 6 whole chillies
- Olive oil for the marinade
- Cracked pepper
- 1 lemon, juiced
- ¼ bunch continental parsley, chopped
- Extra virgin olive oil

Cut spine from spatchcock, and flatten.

Place in a container with bay leaves, chillies and cover with oil to marinate overnight.

Take the spatchcock out of the oil, place on a plate, and then sprinkle an even amount of pepper on both sides. This will impregnate the spatchcock without letting the skin burn; most of it will fall off when you turn the spatchcock.

Place the spatchcock skinside down in a very hot pan and place a pot filled with water over it to press it down while cooking.

Cook each side for 15 minutes, always with a weight on top.

Serve topped with lemon juice, chopped parley and extra virgin olive oil, and a fresh garden salad.

The Mediterranean Diet

Opinions are varied but it seems everyone has something to say about anti-oxidants nowadays. In my view anti-oxidants should come from natural foods—the food we eat and even the beverages we drink should supply a good part of our anti-oxidant needs without resorting to supplements. Four major anti-oxidants are vitamin C, vitamin E, selenium and beta-carotene. Vitamin C is found in citrus fruits and green leafy vegetables, nuts and seeds are full of vitamin E. Garlic is a good source of selenium and tomatoes are particularly rich in beta-carotene.

All these foods play a starring role in the Mediterranean diet. Somewhat surprisingly coffee, that other Mediterranean favourite, also appears to play a role in supplying anti-oxidants.

For years scientists have known that the Mediterranean diet prolongs life and keeps you looking younger too.

One simple rule of eating or drinking is that you have to do it in moderation; smaller meals throughout the day help not only your fitness levels, but do not overload your digestive system, giving your body a chance to work smart. Stay away from fried food, saturated fats, white flour and sugar—these can also be especially bad for your skin.

And, most importantly of all, you must drink water. Yes, pure, simple water and lots of it.

Salmon can be cooked a thousand different ways, but it vital not to overcook it. Whichever recipe you choose, please keep it simple. Apart from looking good on salmon, poppy seeds are known to be an aphrodisiac. For this dish choose a barrel fermented chardonnay with a high level of acidity.

Salmone Atlantico ai papaveri

Atlantic salmon with poppy seeds

Serves 4

- 1kg (2lb) fresh filleted salmon (Atlantic preferred)
- 4 egg whites
- Salt and pepper, to taste
- 100g (3½oz) poppy seeds
- Limes for juice
- 50ml (1½fl oz) extra virgin olive oil
- 8 small potatoes for mash or 220g (7oz) rice
- 4 limes cut into wedges
- snow pea sprouts to garnish

Cut approximately 200g (6½oz) off the salmon and place into a blender or food processor.

Add egg whites and salt, then blend to an even consistency.

With a spatula, coat the whole remaining salmon fillet with the salmon mousse, then an even coating of poppy seeds.

Heat baking dish on the stove and sear both sides of the salmon. Place into a hot oven, 200°C, (400°F) Gas Mark 5 for approximately 5 minutes, cooking until rare.

Cook potatoes to mash or rice.

On a chopping board, cut salmon into four portions, then cut again into 2 or 3 slices. Place each portion over plain mashed potato or boiled rice with snow pea sprouts added last.

Top with lime juice, extra virgin olive oil and freshly crushed black pepper. Decorate with fresh lime wedges. This dish should be served with a fresh green salad.

This dish is a rich source of omega-3 and anti-oxidants—so typical of the Mediterranean diet.

Salmone allo zafferano

Poached salmon

Serves 4

- 2 celery stalks, chopped
- 1 carrot, chopped
- 1 leek, chopped
- Peppercorns
- 750g (1½lb) fresh Atlantic salmon, cut into 4 portions
- 1 bunch asparagus
- 1 Pontiac potato, sliced
- 60ml (2fl oz) sunflower oil
- 1 punnet of cherry tomatoes
- 20g (¾oz) saffron
- 60ml (2fl oz) fish stock
- 1 bunch of basil, shredded (chiffonade)
- Pepper, to taste

Bring to the boil ½ litre of water in a shallow pan, add the celery, carrot and half the leek and a few peppercorns to make a *court bouillon*.

When lightly boiling, poach the salmon for a few minutes.

Also poach the asparagus and sliced potato separately in salted water.

In a shallow frying pan over a moderate heat, heat the oil and sauté the remaining leek, cherry tomatoes and sprinkle over the saffron. Add fish stock and reduce.

On a serving plate, place the potato and then the fish, cover with the asparagus then finish the dish with the sauce, leeks and tomatoes.

Sprinkle with basil and crushed pepper and serve with Funghi al forno (see page 74).

What I like about this dish is that it's quick and easy to cook, and delivers the most elegant flavours. Because of the potato and leek, I like to pair this dish with a wooded chardonnay.

Salmone zafferano e patate

Salmon and saffron

Serves 4

- Extra virgin olive oil
- 800g (1lb9½oz) Atlantic salmon fillet, cut in four portions, seasoned
- Salt and pepper, to taste
- 100g (3½oz) new potato, diced very small
- 1 leek, chopped
- 1 bunch chives, chopped
- 5g (¼oz) saffron
- 100ml (3fl oz) fish stock
- 50g (2oz) butter

In a hot, non-stick, oven proof frying pan, heat oil and sear the preseasoned salmon on both sides. Remove salmon from pan and place in a warm place to rest.

Sauté the potato and leek in the same pan, place the salmon back in, then place pan in a hot oven, 200° (400°F) Gas Mark 5 for 10 minutes. Take out of oven.

Transfer the salmon from the pan to a serving plate.

Place the pan over a high heat, add the butter and chives to the potatoes and leek together with the saffron.

Deglaze the pan with the stock, cook for a few minutes then pour everything from the pan over the fish and finish with pepper.

This dish comes from Capri, an island just off the coast of Naples. It will be familiar to most people who eat out in Italian restaurants—it's also known as veal parmiggiana. I felt I had to include it because it is so much of a staple of Neapolitan cooking. It combines all the ingredients that make southern Italian food distinctive and it's also almost impossible to mess it up.

Scaloppine alla caprese

Veal with eggplant

Serves 4

16 thin slices of veal back strap
Plain flour
Vegetable oil for deep frying
2 medium eggplants (aubergines) cut in 16 slices
16 slices of mozzarella
Salsa pomodoro (see page 85)
1 tablespoon butter
1 bunch of fresh basil
100ml (3fl oz) dry white wine

Tenderise the slices of veal with a mallet so they become thinner, dip them in flour and deep fry them for about one minute on each side. Drain the veal of any excess oil on a paper towel. Slice the eggplant into rings about ½cm (½in) thick, and deepfry them in oil for about 3 minutes until they are golden in colour.

In a flat, flame-proof dish, layer the veal, top with eggplant, mozzarella, salsa, a leaf of basil, a knob of butter and then pour all the wine and the remainder of the salsa over the top.

Place on the stove over a high heat for 5 minutes, giving all the flavours a chance to combine.

Lift out the veal, eggplant and mozzarella on to plates, four per plate, leaving all the sauce in the dish.

Reduce sauce for a further for 3 minutes. Pour over the veal and serve.

Scaloppine al mascarpone

Veal with mascarpone

Serves 4

- 12 slices of veal
- 50g (2oz) butter
- Flour
- 100ml (3fl oz) veal stock
- 100g (3½oz) cream
- 200g (6½oz) mascarpone
- 1 bunch English spinach (silverbeet)
- Shaved almonds
- Pepper, to taste

Tenderise the veal with a meat mallet. Heat the butter in a frying pan over a medium heat, coat the veal in flour and cook on both sides.

Add half the veal stock, all the cream and mascarpone and cook for 10 minutes over a high heat.

Wilt the spinach in the remaining stock in a pan. Either discard the stock or add to the other pan for reduction. Place the spinach on a plate, top with the veal, reduce the remainder of the sauce and pour over.

Sprinkle the dish with the almonds and pepper to serve.

Trippa in casseruola

Tripe casserole

Serves 4

- 400g (13oz) bleached tripe
- 4 bay leaves
- 100ml (3fl oz) olive oil
- 2 carrots, diced
- ¼ bunch celery, diced
- 2 onions, diced
- 6 fresh tomatoes, chopped
- 200ml (6½fl oz) dry white wine
- ½ bunch fresh mint, chopped
- Extra virgin olive oil
- Parmesan cheese, grated

Bring 5 litres of salted water to the boil with 2 of the bay leaves and place the whole tripe in it. Cook for 20 minutes.

Leave in the water to cool down then cut into strips.

In a large casserole, heat oil and cook the diced carrots, celery, and onion, with the remaining bay leaves for 10 minutes, add the tripe for a further 10 minutes over a high heat.

Add the tomatoes and wine, cover with a lid and cook for 40 minutes, stirring occasionally.

Add the mint in the last 10 minutes of the cooking with 2 tablespoons of extra virgin olive oil.

Serve in a deep dish with lashings of grated parmesan cheese, drizzles of extra virgin olive oil and toasted Italian crusty bread.

CHASSEUR

Uccelletti di vitello

Skewered veal

Serves 4

- 100g (3½oz) breadcrumbs
- ½ bunch continental parsley chopped
- 50g (2oz) grated parmesan cheese
- 50g (2oz) butter
- 16 slices of veal back strap, thinly sliced
- 1 onion, sliced
- 12 bay leaves
- 2 lemons, juiced
- Extra virgin olive oil

In a bowl mix half the breadcrumbs, half the parsley, the cheese and the butter.

Tenderise the veal and place the mixture evenly in the middle of each slice then roll it up.

Place the rolled veal on a skewer, followed by a slice of onion, bay leaf and then the veal again, repeating the process until you have four slices of veal on each skewer.

Dip the veal in the remaining breadcrumbs and place over a pre-heated hot plate or large hot pan, grilling on both sides.

Place the veal skewer on a plate, top with the remaining parsley, lemon and extra virgin olive oil.

Serve with green vegetables.

Vitello imbottito

Veal pockets

Serves 4

- 800g (1½lb) 8 slices of veal
- 8 slices prosciutto crudo
- 8 slices of mozzarella
- 50g (2oz) butter
- Oil
- Flour
- 60ml (2fl oz) brandy
- 100ml (3fl oz) veal stock
- 200ml (6½fl oz) cream
- Pepper, to taste

Tenderise the meat with a meat mallet. Place the prosciutto and mozzarella on the veal slices, fold up to create a pocket, and then pound the extremities again with the mallet to seal.

In a frying pan, heat the butter and a little oil, dredge the veal pieces in the flour then sear on both sides. Flame with the brandy, add your stock, cook for 2 minutes then add the cream. Cook for a further 10 minutes, turning the meat once.

Place the veal on a plate, reduce the sauce to a thick consistency, pour over the meat and serve with crushed pepper.

This is a great way to use of alcohol in a dish. Nocello is the nut flavoured liqueur I recommend, but if you can't find it you can substitute with Frangelico. Use different nuts to vary the taste and texture. The watercress is there purely for a light nutty balance. A pinot noir is perfect with this dish.

Vitello aromatizzato

Veal and lavender

Serves 4

- 100g (3½oz) macadamia nuts, chopped
- 8 stems lavender
- 50g (2oz) butter
- 4 x 170g (5½oz) veal fillet, trimmed of all fat and sinew
- 30ml (1fl oz) nut flavoured liqueur
- 30ml (1fl oz) brandy
- 200ml (6½fl oz) veal stock
- 250g (8oz) watercress

In a bowl, mix nuts with chopped leaves of ½ of the lavender.

In a frying pan, heat the butter and add veal fillets, sealing the meat on all sides.

Add the nut and lavender mix to the pan, use a high heat but be careful not to burn the butter.

Deglaze the pan with liqueur and brandy. Add the veal stock and bring to the boil.

Place pan in the moderate oven, 180°C (350°F) Gas Mark 4 for approximately 10 minutes to cook to medium rare.

Remove pan from the oven and rest meat for 10 minutes in a warm place. Place watercress on serving plate, cut veal fillet into slices and place on top.

While the meat is resting, reduce the sauce in the pan over a high heat, stirring frequently.

Pour the sauce over the veal and garnish with remaining leaves of lavender. This dish can be served with a big dollop of mashed potato mixed with some butter.

Desserts

DESSERTS

Biscotti di mandorla

Baked almond bread

6 egg whites
50g (2oz) caster sugar
100g (3½oz) plain flour
200g (6½oz) whole almonds, peeled
Icing sugar

Whisk egg and add sugar till firm, fold in flour and almonds, place in non-stick bread tin and bake for 15 minutes at 180°C (350°F) Gas Mark 4.

Allow to cool then slice thinly. Toast under a grill and serve with icing sugar.

This is an easy dessert to make, the consistency is like a custard. In summer, stone fruit or berries can be added to the bottom to give you the extra texture and flavours of the fruit. You can also serve biscotti or wafers on top.

Mascarpone

Mascarpone custard

4 eggs
250g (8 oz) sugar
500g (1lb) mascarpone
60ml (2fl oz) galliano
60ml (2fl oz) brandy

Separate the eggs, then cream the yolks with the sugar.

Whisk the whites like you would a meringue, and then fold the two together.

Whisk the mascarpone and fold in the egg mixture with a spoon.

Pour your liqueur and brandy over, mix together and serve in a champagne coupe with wafer biscuits.

This is a very similar dessert to tiramisu. It should definitely be served with a good liquer..

Mascarpone al cacao

Mascarpone with bitter cocoa

Serves 4

6 egg yolks
6 tablespoons of castor sugar
500g (1lb) mascarpone
100ml (3fl oz) coffee flavoured liqueur
50ml (1½fl oz) brandy
6 egg whites
6 tablespoons of sugar

Cream egg yolks and sugar, add mascarpone and mix well. Pour in the alcohol and combine.

Whip egg whites, and add sugar. Fold into mascarpone mix.

For Base

1 packet of savoiardi (available from Italian deli)
2–4 cups strong black coffee
Bitter cocoa powder for garnishing

Crush savoiardi and add coffee to form a thick dry paste. Put this at the bottom of your serving dish, cover with mascarpone mix and dust with cocoa powder to serve. Place in the fridge to set for minimum one hour. Dust with cocoa.

Mascarpone reale e parmiggiano reggiano

Cheese with pears

Serves 4

- Crusty Italian bread
- Extra virgin olive oil
- Salt and pepper, to taste
- 100g (3½oz) mascarpone
- 100g (3½oz) gorgonzola
- 150g (5oz) parmiggiano reggiano
- Grissini sticks
- Fresh honey
- 2 hard green or brown pears, quartered and cored

To make the crostini slice some crusty Italian bread or baguettes very thinly, it could even be left over from the day before. Drizzle some extra virgin olive oil, salt and pepper and place under a hot grill to brown on both sides.

Cream the mascarpone and the gorgonzola together to an even consistency and serve on plate with the whole piece of parmiggiano.

To garnish, serve with the grissini, honey in a small container and the pears that have been quartered and cored.

Riso al mascarpone

Rice cakes

Serves 4

1.25L (2 pints) milk
250g (8 oz) arborio rice
50g (2oz) unsalted butter
100g (3½oz) sugar
300g (9½oz) Amaretti biscuits
2 eggs
Flour
Almond flavoured liqueur
Brandy
Vanilla stick

Place the milk in a small pot with the unwashed rice, bring to the boil stirring frequently, and then simmer over a low heat for approximately 25 minutes.

After it is cooked add the unsalted butter and sugar.

Crush the amaretti, and then mix the rice adding 2 eggs and some flour, making the mix dry. Place in a square container, that has been covered in either grease proof paper or aluminium foil, placing in the fridge letting it set for 2 hours.

Cut the rice in large squares, and then dredge it through flour, and egg mixed with brandy, then shallow fry, in hot oil.

This can be served over a thin layer of mascarpone custard (see page 161), sprinkled with icing sugar.

This is a very old recipe from the Amalfi coast of Italy. It should be prepared a week before serving it.

Melanzana al cioccolato

Eggplant in chocolate sauce

Serves 6

- 1kg (2lb) eggplant (aubergine)
- Salt
- Vegetable oil for frying
- 6 eggs, beaten
- 100g (3½oz) sugar
- 30g (1oz) cinnamon powder
- 2 lemons for zest
- 30g (1oz) candied orange
- 30g (1oz) roasted almonds
- 50g (2oz) candied fruits
- 25g (¾oz) bitter chocolate
- 100g (4oz) Amaretti biscuits, finely chopped
- 500ml (16fl oz) milk
- 50g (2oz) bitter cocoa
- 1 tablespoon sugar

Peel and cut the eggplant into thin slices, sprinkle with salt and sit for 1 hour and pat dry. Fry lightly in hot oil. Leave to cool on paper towel.

Dip eggplant in egg and fry each one again. While hot, dip them in the sugar, cinnamon, lemon zest and the candied orange, then leave them to cool down.

Mix together the almonds, candied fruits, chocolate and biscuits in a bowl.

Bring the milk to the boil, add the cocoa and sugar over a slow heat, stirring constantly until firm.

In a 20cm (8in) round dish, place a little chocolate then add the eggplant and the fruit mix in layers. Add up to 3 layers, always finishing with the chocolate.

Cover the dish and place in refrigerator for at least 5 days.

Pere al forno

Baked pears

Serves 4

- 40g (1½oz) raisins, chopped
- 40g (1½oz) stoned dates, chopped
- 40g (1½oz) mixed nuts, chopped
- 6 large brown pears, peeled and cored
- 100ml (3fl oz) red wine
- 1 cinnamon stick
- Sugar
- Pouring custard, to serve

Mix together the raisins, dates and nuts.

Stuff the pears with the mixture and place the pears with the wine and cinnamon in an oven-proof dish. Cover with foil and bake in a pre-heated moderate oven, 180°C (350°F) Gas Mark 4 for 40 minutes.

Take them out of the dish and allow to cool.

Over a high heat, reduce the wine and add a little sugar, until it turns into syrup.

Arrange the pears on a serving dish, pour the syrup over them. Serve with custard.

Tartine di frutta

Plum tart

Serves 4

175g (6oz) butter
175g (6oz) sugar
175g (6oz) almond flour
2 eggs
1 tablespoon vanilla essence
50g (2oz) plain flour
1 large sheet puff pastry
500g (1lb) plums, sliced

Cream the butter and 100g (3½oz) of sugar, and slowly add the almond flour, eggs, vanilla and the plain flour. Work at a slow speed to make the cream, so as not to release the naturals oils of the almond flour.

Lay the puff pastry on a baking tray, pour in the cream, then spread the plums on top. Sprinkle the remaining sugar evenly to achieve a caramelised effect while baking, and place in a pre-heated moderate oven, 200°C (400°F) Gas Mark 5 for 30 minutes.

Serve with fresh cream or ice cream.

2006
piemonte - italia
Cascinetta Vietti
moscato d'asti
denominazione di origine controllata e garantita
ALCOHOL 5.5% BY VOL. - WHITE WINE - 375 ML

Index

Clockwise from top left: *My travel foodie buddies from left Enza and Sandro Capozzi with Gordana Savic. Sandro is my best friend and even at his wedding on the way to the church we stopped at a cheese factory and ran very late for the ceremony. I was his best man. Things have not changed much these days—food is more important than anything else.*
Gordana Savic (also my general manager) and me. This woman has put up with me for a long time.
The Fellini partners: from left to right Enrique Blazquez, Raffaele Di Benedetto, Anna Cacace, Richard Burt Carlo, Bekky Buchanan and Gianluca Percuoco, me, Carlo Percuoco.
My sister Anna, my mother and Carmela.